Open My Eyes

The information contained in this book will change the way you look at the world and may very well save your life.

Published by

IHS Training LLC

54 Chatham Place

Guntersville, AL 35976

www.IHS-Training.com

Printed in the United States of America

ISBN: 978-0-9888660-0-3

Open My Eyes

Travel Safety and Security Information for Christian Mission Trips

Open My Eyes provides practical advice and specific information on what to do in order to keep yourself and your traveling companions safe. This book also teaches you how to identify and avoid the same types of troubles found right here at home. My advice applies as much to everyday life as it does to traveling around the world. Through this book I intend to open your eyes to various types of hazards and dangers often encountered during travel and daily life so that when confronted by it you automatically identify the problem and react properly.

Author: Brian R. Webb

WARNING

The information provided herein is designed for educational use only. It is not a substitute for specific training, experience or good common sense. The author has made every effort to ensure the publication of correct information at the time of printing. IHS Training LLC, and the author assume no liability for any individual's use of or reliance upon the material contained or referenced in these pages. Further, the author disclaims any liability to any party for whatever losses or damages caused by errors, omissions or misleading information found in the pages of this book. When traveling overseas each individual assumes responsibility for proper knowledge, experience and equipment to travel safely. Furthermore, even when an individual acts appropriately sometimes bad things just happen. The advice and information in this book will greatly improve the odds that you will stay safe; however, people sometimes end up in the wrong place at the wrong time. In some cases no amount of training or preparation will prevent bad things from happening.

DEDICATION

I dedicate this book to all the men and women of the Christian faith who leave their homes, families, jobs and other obligations each year to go out into the world to fulfill the great commission serving the Lord.

THE GREAT COMMISSION

Then the eleven disciples went to Galilee, to the mountain where Jesus had told them to go. When they saw him, they worshiped him; but some doubted. Then Jesus came to them and said, "All authority in heaven and on earth has been given to me. Therefore go and make disciples of all nations, baptizing them in the name of the Father and of the Son and of the Holy Spirit, and teaching them to obey everything I have commanded you. And surely I am with you always, to the very end of the age."

Matthew 28:16-20 (NIV)

ACKNOWLEDGMENTS

Publishing this book would not have been possible without the assistance of many people, including my parents, who; from a very early age opened my eyes to exploring the world. Some of my earliest memories are from the years my brother and I spent growing up on a tropical island in the South Pacific. We traveled to exotic locations such as Japan in the mid 1960's at a time when very few Americans had ever visited the country. To my wife who spent countless nights taking care of our children and worrying herself sick while I was away on missions around the world, not to mention supporting my efforts to teach people how to be safe and secure through our seminars.

I also want to express my appreciation to the following people for their assistance in the development of this book and the seminars that IHS Training LLC presents. These include Skip Stoffel, Ralph Wilfong, Peter Kummerfelt, Tim Kneeland, Brett Stoffel, John Burrough, Chris Nevins, numerous dedicated missionaries from around the world, all the mission teams who have provided me with their stories and many others.

FORWORD

One of my great friends told me many years ago, "It's hard to be satisfied with existence once you've tasted Purpose." It was an incredibly strong statement that had a great and lasting effect on me. It forced me to challenge my inner most thoughts, "Do you want to just exist or do you want to live a life of legacy, a life of significance? Do you desire to have an impact on people for good?"

My "Purpose" was found in serving others and it comes from my faith in Christ. Jesus modeled this before he was crucified when He washed the feet of his disciple's at the last supper. The implication was that you are to love one another, and to serve one another. There are many people, all over the world, who feel called to serve others in some form or capacity. They have come to a place in their lives where mere existence just doesn't satisfy the soul anymore.

A person's feeling of being called to serve, or one's willingness to go, has led countless people into stepping out of the safety and security of their homes and traveling to distant destinations on earth to serve others. Many of these destinations lie in foreign countries or regions where common safety and security is not even on the radar screen. Often times these travels lead us to work with the poorest of the poor and those who live and exist in the darkest corners of society. Working or traveling to these locations can be a challenge even if you are prepared, but can turn into a complete disaster if you are unprepared. This is where Brian has stepped in and filled a serious need.

There are many organizations that send mission teams all over the planet without any education, training, or knowledge of how to handle crisis situations and security issues. Brian's teachings on sound travel safety and personal security procedure's gives those going the information needed to operate where the greatest needs are. His crisis management training provides the sending church or organization a greater understanding of how to support those who they send when things don't go as planned.

My belief is that having the training and knowledge that Brian imparts is an absolute necessity! This information is not only for mission teams, but also incredibly useful in day to day life and common domestic travel. I don't say this as a casual observer from afar. I have been through Brian's training multiple times and on each occasion I gain a higher level of understanding and implementation. Whether I am taking teams into Southeast Asia, Haiti, or the Middle East, I have used and implemented Brian's teaching in every phase of travel. From pre-trip planning, to in-country travel and in coming home, the instruction Brian provides has allowed me to become a better, more prepared and more capable leader.

Brian has an incredible heart for God's work, and for people who feel called to go and do His good works. Brian's resume of work includes decades of traveling and operating in and out of some of the most dangerous places in the world. This has given Brian incredible wisdom and experience to draw from in imparting his knowledge. He has instructed countless law enforcement officers, operators from military special operations units, government agency personnel from several foreign countries, and civilians across the country how to survive, how to get in and out of dangerous places, and how to make it back home safely.

Brian provides great, common sense knowledge that will help anyone be a more competent and aware traveler.

Open My Eyes provides invaluable information for any organization engaged in sending mission teams around the United States or around the world. It is also a 'must have' for any mission team leader, any team participant, and any person who is involved in long-term missions work abroad.

This book opens your eyes to a wealth of common sense personal safety practices and travel security knowledge. It gives a person the basic understanding and knowledge to travel to the ends of the earth and be courageously involved in God's work around the globe.

John Burroughs
Director of globalX trips
North Point, globalX
www.goglobalx.org

PREFACE

I consider working with Brian Webb, both personally and professionally for over 18 years, an honor and a privilege. Our interactions in the training arena run the gamut from underwater egress, to academic and practical field training for global survival, up to and including surviving a hostage scenario. My respect for Brian's knowledge, background and professional capabilities in the international travel environment continues to grow along with our relationship. As someone who travels extensively throughout the world, I highlight the uncommon nature (professional or personal) of the information contained in these pages. The strategies and practical suggestions listed will potentially save lives, not to mention the provided peace of mind that goes with preparedness and knowing what to expect in unusual situations.

Preparedness diverges dramatically from convenience! To really make a difference, consider preparedness as an ethic ingrained in daily habits and an ever present situational awareness. The real benefits of preparedness for citizens usually stems from taking a first big step, accepting responsibility for personal welfare and personal safety. Prepared people pay attention to conditions, environments, situations and circumstances with the potential for causing bodily harm. At a personal level, that means walking the walk, talking the talk and following through with sound habits to build both muscle memory and positive mental images.

A fundamental human truth: People tend to act, feel and perform in accordance with their perceived truth about their surroundings, personal well-being and the situations in which they find themselves. This basic concept forms the root cause of countless numbers of bad experiences and life threatening situations encountered by American tourists, business employees, aid workers, and missionaries traveling throughout the world. In essence, they suffer from a lack of preparation (mentally and physically) for what they encounter when leaving our shores. That's why this publication, *Business Travel Safety* and Brian's first book, *Open My Eyes* create a vital foundation for international travel safety and security. These two publications provide one of the most comprehensive sources ever published.

If bad things happen, and sometimes they will, regardless of how well we plan or prepare, keep in mind **knowledge is light to carry!** Armed with the right knowledge, individuals will make the right choices, take appropriate action, create productive, reliable habits and maintain a healthy situational awareness.

Robert "Skip" Stoffel
President, Emergency Response International
Former U.S. Air Force Survival Instructor
www.eri-online.com

Brian Webb spent many years working in a number of capacities for the US government. His duties took him to many parts of the world - some friendly and many not so friendly! In the course of his travels, often alone, his safety was totally dependent on what he did to keep himself safe. *Open My Eyes* captures the lessons he learned while on the road - lessons that kept him safe in some of the world's most dangerous places.

Brian's concise, personal writing style makes this book "an easy read." If you adopt and practice the advice he gives you will be far less likely to have a problem the next time you travel and, should something unpleasant happen, you'll be better equipped to handle it.

It is unfortunate that so many people fall into the trap of believing that nothing bad is ever going to happen to them and if it does, they will be able to muddle through somehow. They believe that if they get into trouble either in the US or overseas, someone is always going to come to their assistance. In the "real world" *bad things do happen to good people and sometimes no one comes to help.* Take responsibility for your own safety - no one cares more about you than you do.

Peter Kummerfeldt
President, Outdoor Safe
Wilderness Survival Expert and former Director of Survival Training at the United States Air Force Academy
www.Outdoorsafe.com

I've known Brian since 2004 when he served as the Director of the Customs and Border Protection (CBP) survival school, Director of Covert Operations and as a federal agent. Brian played a critical role in the design, delivery and evaluation of all survival courses taught to CBP aviators and marine officers.

It quickly became obvious Brian possessed a unique skill set, often putting him into harm's way while performing his duties in some dicey areas of the world. His knowledge of international travel, crime and terrorism is unique and complete. Not only that, but Brian has a real talent for sharing what he has learned with others, as he does very effectively through his new business, IHS Training LLC. His presentations and seminars are well-paced, packed with relevant information and presented in an extremely interesting and captivating manner. He quickly gains and easily holds the attention of his various audiences. In addition to his excellent instruction, Brian is an accomplished author, writing books and classroom materials to support his presentations.

Tim Kneeland
President, Survival Educators
www.survivaleducators.com

As someone who received Brian's training *after the fact*, I strongly urge anyone, traveling anywhere, to read this book and buy a copy for family, friends and travel team members. The information in here may save your life or the life of someone you love. We are thankful that God chose Brian to share his talents in this book.

Christopher M. Nevins
President, Fuel the Mission
www.FueltheMission.org

I don't have time to read another book. Why did you send me such a good book packed with applicable ideas? The only room I had to give up came from my sleep. I don't just "read" -- I write, go back and check, research etc. I'm half way through it and like it a lot. I was up till 10 last night (my family and friends would never believe that) and up again at 2:00 this AM soaking it in.

Thanks for ruining my sleep but keep up the good work anyway.

Carl Chinn
former Building Engineer/Security for Focus on the Family
Speaker and Author: *Evil Invades Sanctuary*
www.CarlChinn.com

INTRODUCTION

I am not a *professional* writer. As a simple man, God has opened some incredible doors for me during my life. I have experienced more in my lifetime than anyone could ever find in the best spy novel. My career in international travel safety and security started in my childhood at the age of 5, when my family moved to Kwajalein, a 3-mile-long island in the South Pacific. Before I even started elementary school I had visited many far-off places with a variety of cultures. Places like Japan and the Marshall Islands, where, in the 1960's very few people living there had seen a blond-haired, blue-eyed Caucasian.

In the early 80's I started a career in aviation and worked for several different airlines. Unfortunately, each of these airlines went out of business after just a few years; however, I was selected to be part of the startup team for one of the airlines from its beginning. Working with the Proving Team, we researched and developed the in-flight emergency procedures that the Federal Aviation Administration (FAA) ultimately approved for airline certification. I helped teach those procedures to other airline employees and passengers.

When talking to mission teams around the country I'm amazed at how many people are traveling out of the country for the first time on a mission trip. In fact it's not unusual to find a number of people attending my seminars each year who have never flown before. When I talk to these people about their fears and concerns, many bring up their fear of flying. Unlike business travelers who consider flying just a normal part of everyday life, many people traveling on mission trips seldom travel by air. I believe God had a plan for me many years ago when He opened that door and placed me in that development position in the new airline. God needed me to gain those skills and that knowledge in order to serve him today.

After my last airline position, flying Boeing jets out of Atlanta International Airport, I was at a crossroad in my career. That's when God opened another door which I jumped through with both feet leading me in a totally new career direction. For 22 years I worked as a Federal Agent and a pilot, first with the US Customs Service, then Immigration and Customs Enforcement (ICE) and finally with the Department of Homeland Security, CBP Office of Air and Marine specializing in international narcotics smuggling and airborne counter terrorism operations.

I started my law enforcement career working along the southwest border of the US. While assigned to the Southwest I spent considerable time working in Central and South America alongside numerous foreign law enforcement agencies. After my identity was revealed during an undercover operation, I was transferred to Puerto Rico and worked the Caribbean and South American sector for several years. I loved my job and where I lived, but God obviously other plans for my life, things He needed me to learn, tasks He needed me to accomplish and skills He needed me to obtain in order to place me where I am today with the ability to teach those traveling around the world serving Him how to stay safe and out of trouble.

In 1995, I suffered a serious on-the-job injury and transferred to the agency's Headquarters and National Training Center. Upon arrival, I took charge as the Director and national program manager of a special operations program and greatly expanded my skills in international travel safety and security.

For the better part of a decade my job entailed managing teams of agents running covert operations throughout the US and numerous foreign countries. Even after transferring out of the HQ Director's position and back to a field office, I stayed active in covert operations. All total during my career I spent nearly 20 years working as an operator and 18 years the program's primary instructor teaching these skills to all US law enforcement and intelligence agencies along with federal agencies from numerous foreign countries.

I specialized in traveling to different countries and working with foreign law enforcement to accomplish very specialized missions, then returning home without *anyone* noticing I was ever there. To accomplish this, I've found the best approach involves identifying the dangers and analyzing the issues that repeatedly get mission teams (or any other travelers) into trouble, and then developing procedures and training on how to recognize and avoid those issues. These same philosophies and techniques are what I have utilized to develop the IHS Training travel safety and security seminars.

The approach I take is to collect data on situations travelers repeatedly run into during mission trips, break it down into categories identifying the problems which could have been avoided and develop specific training on how to first identify potential risks and then how to avoid them. With the assistance of the people noted in the acknowledgements section of this book, years of research and data were collected and countless hours were put into the development and knowledge that is passed on in this book and IHS's seminars.

I started teaching this information with corporate seminars for corporate executives and business travelers back in the mid 90's. In 2013, after much encouragement I was convinced to place the information from my seminars into a written format with my first book, *Open My Eyes,* which was written for the needs of missionary organizations and church mission trips. This book was developed specifically for the issues encountered during mission trips to both metropolitan cities and remote destinations. *Business Travel Safety* was a continuation of my first book and written for the travel safety needs associated with corporate travel.

Several people have told me that the information presented in this book boils down to an immense load of common sense. I take that as a compliment as I've witnessed so many people get into trouble for throwing common since out the window and doing some of the dumbest things imaginable.

We've all let our guard down and made safety related blunders during our travels. I'm no different. Sometimes we get lucky and come home safely, but sometimes these mistakes get people into serious trouble. A good reminder of common sense, easy to incorporate security practices is well worth the time it takes to review. The advice I provide in this book is easy to incorporate into your daily life and can pay huge dividends in keeping you out of trouble.

TABLE OF CONTENTS

IHS TRAINING COURSES and SEMINARS:
Safety & Security for Corporate Executives / Business Travelers
Travel Safety and Security for Mission Trips and Missionaries
Crisis Management and Disaster Planning
Basics of Survival Training
Active Shooter in the Workplace / Church
Airline Crewmember Security Training

IHS TRAINING BOOKS:
Business Travel Safety
Open My Eyes

APPENDIX:
Sample Emergency Action Plan

REFERENCES

SOLOMON'S WISDOM ON SAFETY

"A prudent person foresees danger and takes precautions. The simpleton goes blindly on and suffers the consequences."

Proverbs 27-12 (NLT)

1

Understanding the Dangers

Who is responsible for *your* personal safety and security? Is it the mission trip team leader? Does it rest with your church, the mission's pastor, local police or some security company hired to protect the group while staying in a particular country? Whether you learn it the easy way or the hard way, your safety and security ultimately rests in your own hands! Only you can fully keep yourself safe and stay out of trouble. Even when you follow the lead of an expert in this field, mistakes happen and experts miss things. You maintain the responsibility, not only to yourself but to all those traveling with you to point out anything that looks wrong and to take whatever action is necessary to stay safe.

Don't get me wrong, sometimes even when people make every mistake in the book, go places of known danger with no regard to their surroundings or ignore bad things taking place all around them, nothing happens to them. I've learned from years of experience that God truly does keep his hand on us from time to time. Sometimes there is no other explanation as to why people participating in some of the dumbest, most dangerous activities imaginable make it home safely; however, that doesn't mean that we should live our lives that way. Never intentionally place yourself in dangerous situations without a very good reason to be there!

When I talk to mission's pastors around the country I often hear the word "Probably." "*Probably* nothing's going to happen" or "We've been taking mission trips there for 20 years and nothing has ever happened and it *Probably* never will." Interestingly "nothing's ever happened" only holds true until I get the opportunity to spend some time talking with them about their trips. That's when I start to hear all the little stories about the minor things that occurred to them or their mission teams over the years. Most of the events in these stories turn out to be minor but many could have turned into major crisis situations with the slightest change in circumstances.

I remember talking to one pastor in particular who for many years took mission teams into Togo, Africa. When talking about my seminars he absolutely insisted that his mission teams never hear anything from me or anyone else about kidnappings or hostage survival and wanted no part in educating his teams about safety and security.

Over a cup of coffee he went on to tell me the story about an event in the early 90's when he, his wife and son were living and working in Togo. He said a major uprising took place in the country and the military coup searched house to house killing locals and foreigners alike. They killed his neighbors during the turmoil but he and his family were rescued just in time by the French Foreign Legion and ultimately evacuated out of the country. He and his mission teams have been traveling back to Togo for several years but he feels they have no need for any safety or security training. He never wants anyone to talk to his personnel about subject matter as serious as kidnappings or hostage survival.

When I look at the current political instability of Togo and the surrounding countries, I wonder why this guy deliberately stays so blind to the possibility that this same scenario may happen again at any time. This attitude may lead to one or more of his mission teams being in the country totally unprepared for what they encounter.

Working with church leadership around the country I quite often hear pastors say that "God will keep us safe while we work overseas, we're putting our faith in Him to keep us safe and have no need for safety or security training." To a point this rings true, I do believe that God does sometime watch over people doing the Lord's work. While working undercover in some very remote parts of the world, in places where the drug Cartels controlled everything and where horrible atrocities were taking place all around us, I saw American and British citizens working as aid workers with the indigenous people right in the middle of it and nothing happened to them. I truly believe God protected those people as there was no other explanation as to why they were still alive. I used to think of them as some of the bravest people I'd ever seen. That was until I had the chance to meet and spend time with a number of them. That's when I discovered these people weren't all that brave about where they worked. I found out that most, if not all, simply lacked any awareness of the dangers and atrocities happening around them. Sure they knew vaguely about dangers in the area but many, if not most, truly failed to grasp what took place right in front of their eyes. Unfortunately, some of those people learned about these dangers the hard way.

Chris, the president of a construction ministry comes to mind. Chris is a wonderful man and he, his wife and son lived and worked on a major construction project down in Ecuador building an educational facility[1]. Early one evening criminals took them hostage at gunpoint inside their apartment which was located at the facility. They lost everything with the exception of their lives.

---

[1] www.fuelthemission.org

Several months after this incident Chris told me that during the years they lived and worked in Ecuador they often wondered why every store in the area closed at 5 p.m., locked their doors, closed protective shields over their windows and *every* home in the area was built with 10 to 12-foot-high walls around the property with either concertina wire or shards of glass embedded along the top edges. They knew about the dangers in the abstract sense but after living there for several years without incident, they adopted a complacent attitude about any real trouble as Americans typically do.

Americans, as compared to most other nationalities, easily fall into a false sense of security due to the environments they grow up in. With only a few exceptions, the United States appears to others like a fairytale country. Our streets stay clean and are generally safe and secure. We trust that our police and military will protect and serve our security needs. We've learned to rely on simple door locks and electronic entryway access cards to provide for our safety. Our systems and society generate a false sense of security that we carry with us during our foreign travels.

With just a few exceptions, other countries are not like this. We must take into account and understand the differences in culture concerning the countries in which you work with emphasis on safety and security. Americans particularly need to focus on these differences, pay attention to the security practices of the local population and incorporate those practices into your daily activities. The locals may not specifically talk about their security threats because they have grown up in an area where these threats are simply part of their daily lives and security practices, like closing their shops early and building security walls around their homes have become part of their culture and the way they have been raised. If you have local hosts, talk to them about what you see and listen to what they have to say.

I encourage everyone to serve the Lord anywhere they feel called to go; however, I also encourage everyone to educate themselves on the dangers in each country, even each destination within a country. In addition to avoiding the pre-identified specific dangers for each location, travelers need to develop an *Emergency Action Plan* for when things go wrong. Soldiers never walk into an active war zone without wearing a ballistic vest and having a good evacuation plan. But I hear from people all the time who are traveling into what I know are extremely dangerous places and say they are putting total faith in God for their protection, they need nothing else.

Placing your faith in God is wonderful and more of us should have the faith do that; however, that's like a fireman walking into a burning building without first putting on a fireproof suit and respirator! I think God expects us to use common sense and not place ourselves in danger unnecessarily. We should never go someplace with known dangers without first taking proper precaution's and have an emergency action plan should something go wrong.

Since you're reading this book, it tells me that you want to take safety and security issues seriously. To help, I've included the basics of an *Emergency Action Plan* in the appendix section of this book. It's a good place to start building an Emergency Action Plan and doesn't take long to complete. Should something go wrong during your travels you will know what to do and where to go if you encounter an emergency situation. I highly recommend you carry a copy of your *Emergency Action Plan* with you at all times. The chances that you'll be at your hotel when something happens are small so you need to have this resource with you and available at all times.

The facts about problems encountered during mission trips rarely get published. A number of reasons drive this phenomenon. First, pastors don't want people to know that their mission teams have had issues because:

> (a) they believe it makes the church look bad, as if they didn't take care of their congregation, and

> (b) they fear other people won't want to go on future mission trips.

Therefore, only a small percentage of security issues encountered during mission trips ever gets published; however, if you search the internet and other resources you'll always find a few.

Let's take a look at just a few issues I pulled up on the internet with very little effort. These all occurred in just the past year:

- Michael Louis and Lisa Alphonse were taken hostage from their tour bus while on a mission trip in Egypt.
- John and Wanda Sue Casias from Amarillo, TX were killed in Monterrey, Mexico.
- Two church leaders from California and an Empart church planter were kidnapped in India.
- Two American women from Saint Catherine's Monastery were kidnapped in Egypt.
- Mark Rybinski was killed in Tunisia.
- Bethani Thomas from Clinton, MS was kidnapped during his mission trip in Guatemala.

- 16 High School students and chaperones from Glen Ellyn, IL were robbed during a trip to Columbia.
- Roger Ammons from Cleveland was kidnapped.
- Nancy Davis from McAllen, TX was shot and killed during her mission trip in Mexico.
- Four people from Seattle and California were killed in East Africa while on a mission trip.
- Jim and John Scudder from Little Rock were kidnapped in Kenya during a church mission trip.

These are just a few of the more serious security issues that happened this past year. Many serious issues never get reported and thousands of even less serious problems will also never see daylight. I tell you these things not to scare you; rather, my intent is to make you aware that bad things do happen. We all know of the dangers out there, but before we can start the process of keeping ourselves away from it we have to acknowledge the dangers exist.

In 2011 the Center for Disease Control (the CDC)[2] put out some interesting statistics on international travelers. Keep in mind that these numbers track the business and vacation travelers who actually reported having issues.

The CDC found that out of an average of 100,000 travelers:

- 50% will have some sort of health problem ranging anywhere from Montezuma's revenge to a heart attack or even death.
- 8% will need to see a doctor, either during their trip or shortly after returning home.
- 5% will be confined to a bed during the trip.
- 300 will be admitted to a hospital.

---

[2] www.cdc.gov

31

- 20 will need to be evacuated home by aircraft.
- And 1 person will die. This death could be caused by anything from murder to natural causes.

Although the CDC statistics include all forms of travel, the nature of many mission trips (remote locations, extensive physical activity, working at less than ideal conditions in some of the poorest locations on earth) places many mission teams in an environment conducive to serious problems, certainly more so than the average business man or vacationer staying in a 5-star resort.

For statistical purposes, international aid workers (mission trips fall into this category) have an even higher rate of incidents occurring during foreign travel. In 2008 the Overseas Development Institute[3] reported that the mortality rate of international aid workers exceeded those of the United Nations Peace Keeping troops at the time with over 300 killed, kidnapped or seriously injured while working overseas that year. Relief Web International's[4] statistics back these numbers up: in 2008 there were 278 humanitarian aid workers who fell victim to serious crime to include 60 kidnappings. The numbers for 2009 followed in similar fashion with 290 victims with 94 kidnappings, and in 2010 the numbers were 242 and 87.

The statistics show the consistency of major security issues from year to year but remember that these statistics track the number of cases *reported* which certainly sits much lower than the actual number of incidents. On average, with an estimated 300,000 people traveling overseas on mission trips each year, approximately one out of every 1,000 international aid workers will be killed, kidnapped or

---

[3] www.odi.org
[4] www.aidworkersecurity.org/incidents

seriously injured with thousands more falling victim to much less extreme safety or security incidents.

Does this mean that if you work for a non-profit organization or church involved with missions that sends 1,000 people overseas each year that one will end up dead, kidnapped or seriously injured?   Of course not!   These incidents usually happen with groups of multiple people at one time, like the group of doctors killed in April 2014 while working in Afghanistan or the 6 Lynn University members killed during the 2010 earthquake in Haiti.

I include the statistics in this book NOT to scare anyone away from a mission trip or from doing international aid work.   I simply list them so that the reader develops a realistic view about the fact that things can and do happen when traveling overseas.

Safety and security measures must be addressed during the planning for any mission trip or even for a family vacation. The fact that you are reading this book tells me that you already take these issues seriously.   On the positive side, people who obtain proper training and employ the methods listed in this book will considerably reduce the likelihood that they will end up becoming a victim during their travels or even during their daily lives.

2

Perceptions and Intuition

Are you prepared for what can happen? Regardless of how prepared you are, no matter how much planning and training you've done or how safe you try to keep yourself, sometime things just happen that are outside your control. Without warning you can find yourself in the middle of a crisis situation.

Dana Ver Berg is a personal friend of mine and an absolutely wonderful young lady who suddenly found herself in an unimaginable situation. Dana has dedicated her life to serving God's call to serve others and was in Haiti working at an orphanage with 10 people who were on the last day of their short-term mission trip when the earthquake hit Port Au Prince. Here is an email she sent me just a few days after the event:

Saturday, January 16, 2010

"It's impossible for me to explain to you what it's like being here right now. I never thought that seeing decaying flesh, broken limbs, wounded children, battered heads, and lost limbs would become so normal to me. I never thought I would be one of the 3 main helpers in the amputation of a woman's foot at 1 a.m. last night and I now know what it feels like to not know for sure where my meals will be coming from in the following weeks. Our main staple now is spaghetti, rice and beans. I now understand what it feels like not to be able to bathe whenever I want, and have water accessible at all times. I can't explain to you what it feels like to hear each day that another loved one that's close to us has died underneath the rubble. It's weird saying goodbye to my close friends as they evacuate. Countless deaths have been accounted for.

Today the UN showed up and is camped out at our house for the day with their 5 search and rescue dogs. Their dogs have found two dead bodies so far today in the house behind mine, and that is just the beginning of what they're going to find in these houses. I don't understand why all of our houses, including our orphanages, are perfectly fine with only the outside walls to fix. All I know is that God needed us to be there for all of these hundreds of people that have been brought to our clinic "hospital." It has been such a peaceful place here though, despite everything going on. There is something about the street that we live on and the people on it right now, that is so calm and surreal amidst all of this tragedy. It's incredible.

We know that God is present, and living, and active. He is doing His work among these people, and He is filling them with peace and hope. Even all of those who I have talked to who have lost their best friends, sister's, nieces, etc., are still able to say that they trust in the Lord and know that He is sovereign. Incredible! I praise God that He wanted me here to help the people that I love so much. And for some reason, He has saved me from any injuries from the earthquake, and He has let us be a refuge to all of these people. I wouldn't want it any other way than to be here suffering alongside these Haitians and to be able to relate on a deeper level because we're all experiencing it together. Me and the rest of us who are living here wouldn't want it any other way!

Though terror may go on in the night, though riots may break out, though we're still having aftershocks, though we're not entirely sure where our next food supply will come from once our spaghetti runs out, I know that I have my Jesus, and He is everything I need."

Dana Ver Burg
Childhope International Orphanage[5]
Port-au-Prince, Haiti

I stated earlier in this book that I believe God does truly protect people from time to time and this was the case in Dana's situation. As far as they could see in all directions, not a house was standing, yet the only damage to the Orphanage was that a small portion of the back wall fell down and was quickly rebuilt.

Dana and the others serving at the Childhope Orphanage did everything right. Childhope had operated a food bank feeding program and provided the local population with a basic medical clinic for many years. After the earthquake they immediately set up a make-shift hospital with the supplies they had at the orphanage. They even found an orthopedic doctor walking down the street who had lost his wife and child in the quake, brought him into the orphanage and put him to work helping those in need. There was no hospital to send the injured to. They eventually treated several hundred people after the quake with major injuries, some so severe that their limbs could not be saved requiring amputations with little or no surgical tools and through it all they didn't lose a single patient.

---

[5] www.childhope.org

Immediately after the earthquake I tried to make contact with Dana with no success. As with any major natural disaster all phone systems and cell towers were down or overloaded to the point that they stopped functioning; however, the orphanage had a diesel powered generator and was able to power a satellite based internet service for an hour or so each evening. With this satellite link we were able to relay messages back and forth through emails.

Dana had attended one of my Travel Safety and Security seminars just days before she left for Haiti so she understood the possibilities of what can happen in this type of situation. From a security standpoint, my biggest concern was that the orphanage, because of their food bank and feeding program they obviously had stores of food and supplies on hand and this information was well known by all of the locals (both the good people they had been serving and the bad.) I knew that after approximately 5-8 days the local populous would be out of food and some would be willing to do whatever it took to get it. I relayed a message to Dana regarding my concerns and recommended the employees at the orphanage start to prepare for the gangs of men who would certainly come with some specific recommendations on what they needed to do. This message was passed to the rest of the employees at the orphanage who obviously did a little internet research on the subject during the short periods of time they had at night with internet service.

The internet was the only way the employees working at the orphanage could communicate with the outside world and as you can imagine, they were flooded with emails from friends and family back in America. To alleviate some of the email traffic Childhope set up a blog on their internet website where personnel could post comments about their status and keep people up-to-date with what was happening down in Haiti. The following day several employees posted comments about their security issues:

"It's a shame that one would have to resort to such 'sensationalized' reporting to get a headline portraying the Haitian people as being violent and out of control. It's simply not true. The Haitian people have been wonderful and peaceful. We have NO incidents of violence and everyone we are treating is peaceful and cooperative."

Of course the people they are feeding and treating were being peaceful and cooperative. Their needs were being provided for. It was not those people that I was worried about! Humanitarian aid workers have the kindest of hearts. They are there to serve those in need and that's the way it is supposed to be. The orphanage employee's perception of the Haitian people was based solely on the people they were treating; however, in a crisis situation, you have to realize that not everyone is going to be as peaceful and cooperative as those you are taking care of. Even here in the U.S.A. this will happen. Remember the situation in New Orleans after Hurricane Katrina around various parts of the city and inside the Superdome. Horrendous atrocities took place right here at home.

After reading the Childhope blog I sent Dana another message encouraging her and her fellow employees to take the security issue seriously. The blog the next morning read as follows:

"The Haitian people are incredible. They have been very strong, peaceful and completely cooperative with us under a very difficult situation. There are many stories out there to the contrary but, as always, the news tends to find the few exceptions and then portrays that information as the dominant situation."

Perception! They perceived what they were seeing from the people inside the walls of the orphanage as the way things really were everywhere within the country. They failed to grasp the reality of what was happening or what would happen as the crisis developed. The next day this email came through from Dana:

"Hi Brian,

Well, just as you warned, we had to deal with a gang trying to break in the guesthouse! ... Approximately 20 men with at least one gun tried to break into first, the Guest House and, shortly after, the new home we are setting up for the clinic. In both cases they were scared away by responsive gun fire. They seemed very deliberate about which houses they wanted to hit."

Of course they were deliberate. The guesthouse was where the food for the feeding program had been dispersed to the locals for the past several years and everyone knew it. Well, perspectives change and the following day these posts were included in the Childhope blog:

"Our biggest issue right now is SECURITY. We cannot move forward without it – we're frozen."

"We want to see if we can get Marines here."

The transformation on their blog was amazing to read. Overnight their perspectives went from life is great, the people here are wonderful, to: we need the Marines here for SECURITY protection!

Your perspective on virtually everything in life is based on two basic fundamental principles. It comes from the things you've been taught during your life combined with your real life experiences.

Training comes from all sorts of sources: the things Mom and Dad taught you since birth, what you learned in school or in one of my IHS Training seminars, and even from sources such as educational TV shows and documentaries on the Discovery channel. All of these inputs mold your perception of how you perceive the world to be.

This is combined with your real life experiences: the things you've actually seen, touched and felt. We're all guilty of ignoring our training. Mom and Dad told us to hold onto the handlebars when riding our bikes but most of us eventually let go and tried to ride with no hands, fell, skinned our knees and realized from a real life experience that Mom and Dad were right.

Your perception of the world is much different from how the world really is. People who live in poor, depressed and violent countries have a much different perception of the world than you do. My perception of the world, through my training and the extensive real life experiences that I've had, at times seeing some of the worst humanity has to offer, is probably on the far end of that scale. Somewhere between your perception and mine is closer to how the world truly is. One of the purposes in writing this book was to help Americans, who are heading out into the far reaches of the world, understand through training what the world is truly like before finding out the hard way through some real life bad experience!

One of my goals both in writing this book and doing my seminars is to help people recognize the clues when danger is present. Through training on specific issues, people learn what to look for, how to identify the danger signals and learn to trust their intuition. When you get the feeling that something is wrong but don't quite know what it is, trust your intuition! If you truly pay attention to the information in this book the danger signals should sound automatically and you will be able to take quick action to avoid the dangers before they become a problem. Employing the safety and security methods as outlined in this book will make you a MUCH safer person as you walk through life, not just during foreign travels but as you walk through everyday life.

Many people think that if you hear about all the dangers in the world that you'll walk around scared the rest of your life, but just the opposite is true. With proper training and awareness of the dangers you will not only be safer but it will be possible to live life nearly free of fear! When you know what to look for and don't see it, you have no fear. When you know what to look for, your brain will automatically take note of it before you walk into the middle of the dangerous situation and let you know that something is wrong. We often call that intuition. You'll stop, walk around the danger and keep yourself safe and out of trouble.

I've talked enough about statistics and understanding that there really are dangers out in the world that need to be taken seriously. In addition to overseas travel I want to make sure you understand that the information in this book should be applied to everyday life in the same way it does during your travels. The information and the security practices outlined in this book should be incorporated throughout your everyday lives here at home too.

Now that you understand that there are issues we need to be aware of, we can move on and get into the meat of the information and start providing you with a laundry list of specific items to look for and practices to employ that will help improve your safety, security and prepare you for your next mission trip, business trip or overseas vacation.

3

Pre-Travel Preparations

As I get into the heart of this book I will start with the basics and work my way up. As an example, when I get into the chapter on airline safety, I will start with clearing TSA security inspections and end with terrorist hijacking situations! I've talked to dozens of people who have traveled on mission trips and then laid out everything they would be doing from start to finish in an organized fashion. I've addressed the areas where people had worries and concerns along with all of the safety and security advice I could provide within the confines of this book. So let's start at the beginning.

There are a number of items that every traveler needs to consider even before getting to the packing stage of any trip. Some of these items need to be accomplished weeks or even months before your departure date.

If you have a Will or Legal Trust, before leaving on your overseas trip is a good time to go through them and make sure that everything is in order and reads the way you want. Many people with Wills haven't updated them in decades and things in life change. It's always good to take a look at your Will or Trust on a periodic basis and consider updating them every few years.

If you are traveling out of the country someone should have a signed Power of Attorney to take care of you should something tragic happen while you are away in the event you are not able to make decisions for yourself. This can be made in a limited form for just the duration of your trip. A Power of Attorney needs to be written and left with someone you trust, your spouse, a relative or maybe even your best friend before leaving home.

A similar item to have in place is a document giving someone signature authority on your bank accounts (yes, it needs to be someone you really trust!) or you should have a joint account. I've seen people run into problems overseas such as a major injury or illness and many, if not most hospitals in foreign countries run on a cash basis only. If you don't have enough cash on hand to pay the bill, you can have this person put money in your account to get you home.

This situation happened recently with my brother. He was in Geneva on vacation when he was involved in an accident and ruptured his spleen. His insurance company told the hospital that they would cover his medical charges after the hospital filed the claim; however, the hospital refused to let him out of their care until the bill was paid in full. Fortunately our mother had signature authority on his bank account and was able to transfer money into his account so that he could pay the bill. He continued his vacation and was able to settle up with his insurance company for the reimbursement after he returned home.

I also recommend that you contact your medical and life insurance companies to see if they provide coverage in the countries you plan to visit. In addition, write down and keep a list of the company's international phone numbers with you during your travels. This is good information to know ahead of time! Most people don't realize that with very few, if any exceptions, life insurance policies won't pay a dime if you are killed while traveling in a country that has an active State Department Travel Warning[6].

---

[6] www.travel.state.gov

Many if not most places people travel on overseas mission trips have an active travel warning.

If your church does not already provide it, consider purchasing travel insurance before you leave home. This is a good item to look into if you feel you might have the need and depending on how much you travel outside the country and what countries your personal medical insurance covers, travel insurance can be well worth the price. Travel insurance policies are not that expensive. Most run around a few hundred dollars per year. Make sure you check the specific policies each company offers to ensure they include two key functions: Medical and Political Evacuations. Some do, some don't and the price will be virtually the same. If you suffer a major injury or illness in a foreign country you want to make sure that your insurance provider will get you out and into a place where proper medical care can be obtained.

Another item you want to obtain a week or more before you leave home is $200-$300 in the local currency for the country or countries you plan to visit. Some people wait until they arrive and then try to get money out of an ATM, but those are not always readily available. The kiosk at the airport is probably the worst place to make a money exchange and your bank here at home is probably the best. Contact your bank a few weeks before your departure date let them know where you are going and how much local currency you would like to have. Most banking institutions can get you the denomination for that country within a few days to a week and the exchange rate will be very reasonable.

Fair warning for those of you who use your local US cell phone to make calls or even send text messages in a country other than the United States!!! The rates can run as high as $20-$40 per minute (no, I am not joking!) Until recently the only option for overseas travelers was to purchase a World Wide GSM cell phone and a GSM card for the phone. These are still good options and have reasonable rates in the $2-$7 per minute range; however, in recent years a number of cell phone companies have been following Vonage and offering short-term International contracts that can be added to your current coverage. These short-term overseas agreements generally provide very reasonable rates for overseas calls. I recommend that at least one person in your group contact their cell phone carrier to see if they provide service in the countries you plan to visit along with a short-term international contract rider.

Another option for churches that send mission teams into remote field locations is purchasing a Satellite phone. These phones can be purchased for under $2,000 with very low monthly contracts and rates as low as $0.50 per minute. The Inmarsat/Iridium phones will work "anywhere" in the world. During a crisis like the earthquake down in Haiti, satellite phones are probably the only way an organization will be able to communicate outside the country. I also recommend purchasing a solar charger for the satellite phone as there may not be power to recharge the phone depending on the circumstances or where your mission teams travel. If you are sending out numerous mission teams, just hand the phone to each team leader and have them return it at the end of the trip.

For smaller churches that have mission teams traveling into the more remote areas, a number of companies are offering rental Satellite phones. This may be a good option to consider. Depending on where you intend to travel, renting and taking a satellite phone with you could actually be cheaper than purchasing an overseas cell phone contract, if you can even get cell service where you're going.

I recommend contacting someone in the country and even in the specific area you intend to travel and inquire about the availability and reliability of cell phone service before you leave home. You'll find that many underdeveloped countries actually have very good cell phone systems. These countries built their communication infrastructure after the land line systems became all but obsolete, so many countries actually skipped the land line phone systems and migrated directly to cell towers and wireless systems.

How many credit cards do you need to take with you on an overseas trip? The short answer is two. One credit card that you keep with you to use for daily purchases and the other card needs to stay locked or at least hidden away back at your hotel. That way if one credit card gets stolen you can call the credit card company and put an immediate stop on the account and you will still have another card available to use during the remainder of your trip.

Should this happen, who do you call to stop any future charges on the account and what information will you need? It's all listed on the back of your credit card which of course is now in the hands of someone else being used to rack up as many purchases as possible before the bank places a freeze on the account. Before leaving home you need to write down your credit card numbers, expiration date and 3-digit security code (the one on the back) along with the *international* phone number for the bank and keep that information in a safe place, like back at your hotel and a copy with your spouse back in America. This way you will have access to the information after the card is stolen.

49

Some people write their expiration and security codes down backwards or in a code, like being one digit higher for each number (something they can remember) so that this information is not compromised if obtained by someone else. Others place the information in their phones which are password protected or some simply take a picture of their credit cards, both front and back, and email it to themselves. That way, even if they've lost everything they can go to any computer, log into their email account and access the information. Regardless of where or how you store the information, you need to be able to contact your credit card carriers ASAP in order to stop any charges from being placed on a stolen credit card.

Additionally, you need to/must contact your credit card companies before you depart and advise them of your travel plans. Many people forget to do this and after the second or third purchase overseas the bank's computer system will put an automatic lock on the account which can be very difficult to remove in a timely manner, especially from some foreign location. When you inform your credit card company about your impending foreign travel many companies, such as Master Card, will often issue you a new card containing an international chip for overseas travels. Call well in advance and let the bank know where you are going, when you'll be back and ensure your credit limits are sufficient so that should you have an issue and need to either pay a hospital bill or purchase an airline ticket home you are able to cover the costs. A few thousand dollars more than you intend to spend needs to be included in your credit limit to cover any unplanned emergency costs.

People who travel on mission trips usually do more exercise, walking, toting heavy luggage and working on projects than they have done in years. Untold numbers of people have suffered muscle or joint injuries and heart attacks during mission trips. Several months before you leave home "everyone" should start an exercise program to get their bodies used to the additional exertion. At a minimum, everyone going on an overseas mission trip should be walking a mile or two each day!

If you have any known medical problems make sure they are taken care of before you depart. Even simple head colds can turn into major sinus infections by flying which can greatly compound the issue. And if you require any special medications, especially if the medications are something you cannot do without like blood pressure meds or insulin, take an additional seven to ten days' worth of the medication with you than you expect to use.

In 2010, volcano eruptions in Iceland shut down all airline flights over Europe and the Atlantic Ocean. I received calls from numerous clients asking for advice on what to do. These churches had mission teams in places such as small African countries with people who had run out of their medications and were not able to find them locally. This can be a life threatening situation and can easily be avoided by just taking along more than you need. You may need to contact your insurance company about where you are going and request your next month's prescription, or you may need to have your doctor write you a prescription and pay to have it filled. Most insurance companies will permit one additional prescription fill per year if you call them and let them know you are traveling overseas.

Almost all prescriptions can be filled two to three days early. You never know when something will happen even here at home where you won't be able to get your prescriptions filled so I recommend that people fill all of their prescriptions a couple of days early and save the extras. This way you slowly build an emergency supply to have on hand for unexpected situations. Filling and keeping the extras each month will result in your having a full month's supply of your prescription medications on hand at the end of ten months to a year (and it won't cost you a penny.)

I am often asked about medications and vaccinations for overseas travel. The World Health Organization and the Center for Disease Control (CDC)[7] are both good sources of information about disease and medication issues for foreign countries. Medical travel clinics are located in just about every mid-sized city and have lists of vaccinations that may be required or requested for each country you intend to visit. Travel clinics are generally the best source for obtaining these vaccinations and a list of travel clinics can be found on the CDC website.

The last thing I'll cover in this chapter are dental issues. I have been in a foreign country with a partner who had a known dental problem before we departed and have seen how serious a dental problem can be. He had broken a filling and cracked a tooth several days before our departure and, untreated, it turned into an abscess the first week into our trip. After a few days in this foreign country his whole face began to swell. 24 hours later he was in terrible pain and in serious medical trouble.

I'll never forget watching as he tried to communicate with a local dentist who couldn't understand a word my partner was saying, about the issue and what needed to be done. It's a sight I'll never forget and a permanent reminder to take care of any dental problems before you leave home!

---

[7] www.who.int and www.cdc.gov

4

Packing and Items to Take

Before you even start to pack the first item into the suitcase it's a good idea to go through and sanitize items such as your wallet or purse. Remove the items you are not going to need during the trip, things like the grocery store discount cards, Costco or Sam's Club cards, any credit cards you won't be using and you certainly don't want anyone to get hold of your social security card. These items, if lost or stolen, can be a lot of trouble to replace so if you won't be using them, leave them at home!

There are a few items that you specifically want to leave at home that won't be found in your wallet. Specifically, you want to leave at home a copy of your itinerary, not just for your mission trip but for any travels. When the whole household is going on a family vacation, leave a copy of your itinerary with a trusted friend or at a minimum leave a copy sitting on the kitchen table. That way if you don't show up at home when you are supposed to, someone will start to wonder why and they will have a place to start looking for you. If you simply do nothing more than leave a copy on the kitchen table, hopefully your neighbors will call the police and report you missing after the weeds in your yard get out of hand. They in turn will come to your house, enter and hopefully find the itinerary you left sitting on the kitchen table. From this they can call the airline or hotel to determine the last place you were and if necessary start a search to locate you.

A few items that you should always take with you include: a filled prescription for Cipro, at least one water purifier for the group and all of the prescription medications that you'll need for the duration of your trip.

Cipro (Ciprofloxacin) is the medication you need to kill the parasites, those little organisms that get into your gastro intestinal system when you drink the water. Some people call it Montezuma's Revenge (extreme diarrhea) which is similar to Giardia. It strikes a large percentage of travelers and even the most careful travelers will have issues with diarrhea at some point in their travels. To say it can ruin a great trip would be an understatement. Cipro will kill those amoebas, along with everything else in your system, stop the diarrhea and get you home. If you get sick take the Cipro followed by several days of active culture yogurt to replace the good cultures your body needs for digestion.

In many countries Cipro is an over the counter drug but don't count on finding it after you become sick. In fact you might not be able to leave the toilet long enough to get to a pharmacy! Before you travel overseas see your family physician, tell the doctor about your travel plans and have them write you a prescription for the drug, get it filled and take it with you. Even if you don't need it, someone on the trip probably will.

I mentioned taking a water filter with you. I highly recommend that someone in your travel party carry a water filter. I use them in my hotel room even when the hotel says their water is safe to drink. I've been in some countries where the hotel clerk said that their water was filtered and safe to drink only to go into my room, fill a glass with their water, then hold it up to the light and be amazed at what I found swimming in that glass. One trick I use to avoid getting sick is to place one cup in the sink and fill it with tap water, place another cup on the counter and then use my water filter to pump clean water from one glass into the other. Regardless of how clear it is I know that the water in the second glass is perfectly safe to drink.

It may take a few extra seconds to accomplish this task but if you've ever been sick in a foreign country you understand that the time is well worth taking.

One of the first tasks I like to accomplish when I arrive in a foreign country is to go to the nearest pharmacy or grocery store and purchase a case of bottled water. I use the bottled water for everything from drinking to teeth brushing; however, it may be the second day after arrival before I can get to the store to purchase bottled water. That's where the water filter comes in handy.

Some things to watch out for, especially in restaurants, are the ice cubes and fresh salads that have been washed with local water. These two items have gotten even the safest of foreign travelers sick. I avoid the salads and ask for any drink I order to be served in a bottle and brought so that I can open it at the table.

Another reason to carry a water filter is for the slim possibility of a natural disaster. Referring back to the story of my friend Dana down in Haiti, in one of my emails to her I stated that I was really glad she had taken my advice and brought with her a water filter. Her reply was that no, she had not purchased one because it wasn't needed. The Orphanage had its own well which was powered by the generator and they had a large gravity-fed water filtration system that took care of their needs.

Two weeks later Dana sent me another message stating that they were out of diesel fuel and were desperately trying to find some. The next day she sent another message stating that she wished she had taken my advice and purchased a small hand-held filter system! Without diesel fuel they had no way to run the generator and without power, of course they had no way to pump water from the well into their gravity-fed water filtration system. One cheap hand-held unit could have provided potable water for everyone at the Orphanage.

These small hand-held water filtration units like you would use for a backpacking trip are very good to have here at home just in case there is a major problem. I keep one of mine in my vehicle and have been out in the woods on a number of occasions when I was delayed, ran out of water, found a small pond or creek and that little filter was a life saver. Any good sporting goods store will have backpacking filters starting under $100.

The best filter I've found that literally has the best filtration in the industry, is the Pre-Mac system offered by Emergency Response International (ERI)[8]. In fact everything ERI sells on their equipment sales page is not only top quality but I have personally tested each item in the field and everything they sell can be counted on to work in a survival situation!

Another unit I often carry is the LifeStaw[9]. These filters have no working parts and basically work like a straw where you place one end of the unit in the water source and pull water through the filter directly into your mouth by sucking on the other end. They are small, extremely light weight and at just under $20 they are cheaper than any unit I've found; however, if you already have a portable water filter don't buy a new one, just take what you have!

Many mission teams are required to take expensive tools with them during mission trips. Whether it's testing

---

[8] www.eri-online.com
[9] www.lifestraw.com

equipment, specialty tools to help repair or build a facility, medical equipment or dental tools, many items due to their shape and size may not be permitted onboard the cabin portion of the aircraft. Make sure you pack all of your tools in your checked luggage. I've seen people with very expensive sets of screw-drivers or specialty tools lose them during TSA security screening when the agent removed the items from their carry-on bag and threw them in the disposal bin. Simple things that you would never expect like the probes on an electrician's meter can be removed by TSA as you clear security for your flight. This advice applies to anything that may be prohibited to include liquids and any sharp metal item. Just about anything can be carried in your checked luggage but items in your carry-on baggage are very restricted.

One thing you don't want to take is anything truly valuable. Even when you pack these items in your checked luggage, there is a good chance that it won't make it to your destination. I've seen women on mission trips wearing 2-karat diamond wedding rings and diamond stud earrings. These items always need to be left at home. In fact, I recommend you leave all of your jewelry at home. It just makes you more of a target and to be quite frank, if you can't remove the item quickly (I've seen wedding rings that won't come off) thieves in some countries will just as quickly remove your finger to get the ring rather than wait 30 seconds to see if you can get it off. If you really must wear a wedding ring I recommend that you buy a very cheap band from a pawn shop or better yet a cheap plated ring from a local store like Walmart or Kmart. Make sure to get one that is a little loose so that you can take it off easily and give it to any robber who may take a fancy to it. Other items people carry that make them a target for thieves are those very expensive SLR cameras with large telephoto lenses. These are valuable items on the black market overseas and are often stolen at gun-point or knife-point. Some of the new, smaller digital cameras take very good pictures, cost around $100 and if stolen are no huge loss (with the exception of the pictures you've taken).

Something I do recommend you include on/in each bag you take, are two I.D. tags. One as required on the outside of the bag where a conveyor belt may snatch it off and the other located on the inside of the bag where it can be easily seen as soon as the bag is opened. US air carriers are supposed to open the bag before it goes to the auction house for lost and unclaimed luggage in an attempt to try and identify the owner and then return the bag. It may be a month or more after your trip and you've probably replaced everything in the bag but it is nice to get your belongings back.

Regardless of how much you packed in your checked baggage I always recommend you carry a small backpack or carry-on bag with a few essentials. These include:

- A change of clothes (shirt, socks and underwear) to carry you over until your checked bag that got lost shows up or your items can be replaced.
- Your toiletries (at least the basics like a tooth brush, tooth paste, deodorant and razor).
- Any medications you may need. It's amazing to see people who desperately need medication for medical issues like diabetes or heart problems panic when their checked bag doesn't show up. If you truly require your meds keep them in your carry-on!
- Last are your travel documents. I've seen people arrive at the counter where you clear Customs in a foreign country trying to dig their Passport or Visa

out of their checked bag. Keep these items with you on the plane! Travel pouches worn around your neck or waist work well for these documents.

What should you wear when traveling on a plane? Something comfortable of course but believe it or not, what you wear could actually make a big difference in your survival rate should something go wrong during the flight. You should always wear non-descript, protective clothing. This includes the following:

- Long cotton pants (loose fitting blue jeans are probably the best)
- A cotton shirt
- Lace-up shoes (*not* slip-ons, sandals or flip flops)

One of the worst things you can ever wear from a safety perspective is a nylon running suit and flip flops. The second worse thing would be synthetic shorts and sandals or flip flops. As a professional pilot I acknowledge the fact that flying is one of the safest forms of transportation you'll ever take. In fact, statistically speaking your flight is probably the safest part of your entire trip; however, when things do go wrong, they go very wrong in a hurry. These clothing items provide absolutely no protection during an accident. In fact wearing synthetic clothes, flip flops or sandals can actually reduce your odds of surviving.

Let's take the nylon running suit for example. We've all seen people wearing them in the airports and, yes they are quite comfortable but how many of you have ever cut the end of a nylon rope? For those who have, you know that the end will fray and to remedy this issue you simply hold the frayed end up next to a match or cigarette lighter. Within seconds the end of that nylon rope will melt into a bubbling goo. If you've ever made the mistake of making even the slightest skin contact with that bubbling nylon goo you find out very quickly that it will instantly melt right through your skin.

People involved in an airline accident who were wearing nylon running suits have died or suffered horrendous physical burn injuries from these suits literally melting into their skin. In fact you don't even have to touch the flames, the heat from just running past the fire can melt the thin material right into your skin. The same issue holds true for most synthetic materials such as rayon, polyester and those spandex type of stretchy materials, just to name a few. Cotton clothing such as blue jeans and cotton shirts will char when exposed to a flame but they don't melt. They provide a relatively good layer of fire protection for a common, comfortable material to wear.

I'd like you to also take this clothing safety concern outside the airline industry. These same synthetic materials have caused countless devastating injuries to people cooking marsh mellows and hot dogs around the back yard campfire. When you see someone wearing these synthetic materials and standing close to the campfire, please ask them to step away from the flames.

Similar types of issues are present for people wearing sandals or flip flops. Think back to the picture that is usually associated with TV newscasts about a bad automobile vs. motorcycle accident. They show the victim's shoe sitting on the side of the road. That's because, when the victim's arms and legs are flailing around during the accident, the shoes come flying off. Many people have died in aviation accidents because they lost their shoes and could not walk or run through the jagged metal, flames and broken glass in their bare feet. Having lace-up shoes (tennis shoes work well and are very comfortable) can prevent this safety issue should you ever be involved in an accident. If the crew ever says they have a problem and are preparing the cabin for a possible rough landing, one of the first things I would do would be to pull my shoe laces up as tight as I can get them! I want to make sure that my shoes stay on my feet just in case they are needed to get me out of a bad situation.

What part of your airline flight do you think is the most dangerous? Is it the take-off or the landing? No, it's neither of these. The most dangerous part of any airline flight is actually the drive home! Seriously, you are much more likely to be involved in an automobile accident driving home from the airport than you are an airline accident. During that drive home, when you are exhausted from a long overseas flight, is by far the most dangerous part of your journey. But of course, when accidents happen in an airplane they are generally much worse than the average car wreck.

5

Aviation Safety and Security

US Air Carriers have an outstanding safety record in the world of aviation but many overseas trips require you to fly on local commuter planes, in some foreign country, with local pilots whose equipment and training may not be to the same standards as they are here in the United States. Additionally, the airports you'll be landing at may be quite different from those here in the US so in this chapter I will be covering a vast volume of airline safety information. Some of this information you have probably heard before but ignored, and I will include a lot of information that you've never heard before or even thought about. All of the information in this chapter is really good to know and will change the way you fly. Can I guarantee that you'll survive an airplane crash by employing the practices listed in this chapter? Of course not, but I can guarantee that your odds of surviving will go up significantly.

Airline passengers need to show up at the airport a good hour and a half before any domestic flight in order to check in, check your bags, clear the TSA security screening lines and make it to your departure gate before boarding time. If you are traveling internationally on an airline you need to show up at least two hours before your departure, even at the smaller airports. This may seem like a lot but it really is not considering the consequences of being late. Ticket counter lines can be unexpectedly long for international flights and they always take considerably more time to check in each passenger for an international flight than those for a domestic flight. The ticket agent must check each passenger's travel documents before providing them a boarding pass and enter all of their document data into the airlines computer system. This takes time.

For international flights each airline is required to submit an electronic airline passenger information system (eAPIS[10]) manifest to the Transportation Security Administration (TSA) a minimum of one hour prior to departure. The eAPIS manifest lists every passenger who has checked in for that flight, with all of their document information so that government officials can check each passenger against the No-Fly list. If a passenger has not made it through the ticket counter line and presented their documents to the agent 60 minutes prior to the flight, they are not going on that flight! I've seen passengers become outraged at ticket agents over being told that they cannot board their flight when they show up 55 minutes prior to departure, but it's not the airlines' fault. The rules are the rules, TSA's rules, so please show up early (2 hours minimum) so you will make it to your destination on time.

I've even seen passengers think they could outsmart the system in order to save time and get caught by this rule, which doesn't apply to domestic flights. They will print their boarding passes at home, check their bags curb-side in front of the terminal and then go park their car, bypass the ticket agent and head directly to the TSA security screening checkpoint and then go straight to the departure gate. The problem is that if they don't get to the gate, through the line at the counter and present their travel document to the gate agent, who must have enough time to enter their date into the eAPIS manifest 60 minutes prior to departure, they are not going on that flight. Even if the plane is still at the gate and the airline hasn't even started boarding the flight! Again the rules are the rules, TSA's rules, so leave early and make sure you've given yourself plenty of time for unexpected delays.

---

[10] www.eapis.cbp.dhs.gov

Long before heading to the TSA security checkpoint make sure that you are not carrying any prohibited items such as pocket knives, multi-tools or oversized liquids. This only delays you and everyone behind you. I've seen passengers get pulled into secondary screening for having some of these prohibited items in their carry-on luggage which can really delay the passenger from making their flight.

Considering carry-on items, how many of you travel with a laptop computer? Most of us who travel on mission trips rely on our laptop computers for just about everything and many of us couldn't do our jobs without them. Having a computer can also be a good idea in order to check flight statuses, weather and communicate with friends and family back home (Skype is a secure, cheap way to talk with people at home from overseas if you have internet service.) Something to consider as you walk into the airline terminal is that criminals operating in airports have turned laptop thefts into a full-time booming business.

How many laptop computers do you think are stolen in US airports each week? Believe it or not the estimated average is that there are around 10,000 laptop computers stolen each week in US airports[11]. This is a full-time thriving business, stealing computers in airports and then selling them on internet sales and auction sites or on the black market. These thefts can be prevented by following just a few simple practices.

First and foremost is to always keep an eye on your laptop. Many of these computers are stolen from bathrooms, reaching under the stall and snatching them while you have your pants down (no pun intended.) Another ploy takes place while you are seated at the gate waiting for your

---

[11] www.pcworld.com/article/147739/article.html

flight. Thieves will simply pick up your laptop case when you are not paying attention and walk away into the crowded terminal. By the time you realize it's gone, it's too late.

Another common method for stealing computers starts as you enter the airport terminal or are standing in line at the ticket counter. These thieves work in teams of two and specifically look for people carrying those expensive laptop computer cases. If you are carrying the case then you're probably carrying the charger and all sorts of other related items contained in a single location which makes for a great package to steal. These people are professionals and will discretely follow you as you make your way toward the security check point and without your knowledge will slip in line directly in front of you. That's where they work as a team to make the snatch.

The first person in line will have nothing metallic on their body at all as they walk through the metal detector, nothing more than an I.D. and a boarding pass which was printed off a computer and is most probably a fake. The second person will have every type of metal on his or her body they can think of: belts, change, watches and metal items inside pockets that he has "forgotten" to remove. The first person in line will walk right through the security screening without a problem and then hang around the conveyor belt where everyone picks up their carry-on luggage after it has been X-rayed and examined. The second person will delay a little bit until you have placed your computer case on the conveyor belt, then they will walk through the metal detector only to have it go off. Of course the security personnel will have them back up (delaying you) and empty their pockets into the bucket before trying again. This time the metal detector will go off again because of something they've forgotten to remove. Meanwhile the first person in line will be discretely watching you, waiting for that moment when you are distracted by the inconsiderate, metal alarm bandit before casually picking up your computer case and walking into the terminal. It only takes a second or two and by the time you've made it through the screening and to the carry-on pick-up point, your computer case, laptop and all of your important files are long gone!

The good news is there is a very easy way to defeat both of these computer theft scenarios. Carry your laptop in the back section of the small backpack you'll be carrying (as discussed in the packing section) with your extra clothes, medications and travel documents. Most laptops fit very nicely in the back section of the average small school book size backpack. If you have a protective sleeve, place the computer in the sleeve and then slide it into the backpack. If you travel a lot, a great option is to purchase one of the new computer backpacks that have a protective sleeve built into the unit along with file folders and sections with storage slots for all sorts of office supplies.

The trigger key for the computer thieves on all of the methods mentioned above is that nice computer case you are carrying. That nice Dell, Toshiba or Apple computer case is what makes you the target for this crime. They are not looking for someone carrying a small backpack filled with a book, toiletries and extra clothes. I always travel with my computer in a backpack to keep it and my files safe. This is also a great solution for the personal items I need to carry. Of course the move toward tablet computers changes this scenario as they can be carried in just about anything.

The best security for your laptop is to leave it at home! For many mission teams and business travelers this is not an option but when you are on personal travel, if you have a smart phone you generally won't miss it. Just use your smart phone for text and voice, keep the data off unless you have WiFi access and make sure you register your trip with your cell service provider before you leave home. You will generally find internet cafes and computers in most major city hotel lobbies.

I have a saying, "a laptop will get you killed and a smart phone will only get you beat up." In foreign countries people who are carrying nice laptop cases are generally wealthy men or women who are either carrying money or they are very valuable to their companies.

Now that you've moved on past the ticket counter, security screening checkpoint and into the actual aircraft, let's take a look at some interesting statistics about airline accidents.

Approximately 76% of passengers who are involved in an airline accident survive the actual crash in fair shape. Those aren't bad odds, nearly 3/4 of people live through the crash; however, only 42% actually escape without dying or suffering major life-threatening injuries[12]. There are a number of reasons for this but a large percentage of these deaths and injuries can be prevented by following a few simple practices which I will discuss in this chapter.

The number one cause of deaths and major debilitating injuries during airline accidents from people who survive the impact but die before getting out of the plane is from smoke inhalation. The toxic fumes that build up inside the cabin during and even prior to a fire can severely damage

---

[12] www.ntsb.gov

the lungs and there are a number of things you can do to help prevent these inhalation injuries. First and foremost is to stay below the smoke. This sounds simple but smoke, being warmer than the surrounding air, rises and fills the top of the cabin first. During or should I say after the initial impact of an accident, survivors jump out of their seats and race towards the front door where they entered the aircraft in order to get out (regardless of where the nearest exit is located). We've all seen how congested the aisles get when the plane pulls up to the gate and the seatbelt sign is turned off. Everyone stands up in the isle, shoulder to shoulder, and can barely move. Can you imagine how packed the aisle is during a panic situation? Many people get stuck standing in the aisle, unable to move and as the top of the cabin fills with smoke and they are trapped in that location with no option but to inhale those toxic fumes.

To start with the basics, if the cabin is filling with smoke try to stay as low as possible, underneath the level of the smoke. Another item that will help with smoke inhalation is to create a filter to breathe through. Take a piece of cloth, the seat cushion or that extra T-shirt you placed in your backpack, wet it if at all possible and breathe through the filter you've created. Many of us remember the TV images of the survivors running out of the World Trade Center buildings before they collapsed with a ring of black soot around their mouth and nose. That was caused by the moisture in their breath allowing the soot and fumes they were breathing in during their escape to adhere to their face. Any type of filter material will help extend your life.

Another issue is the ignition or flash point of that smoke. Just like gasoline, it's the fumes that will ignite first, not the liquid. If you've ever watched the videos from the inside of an aircraft during a staged accident, after the crash the cabin will fill with smoke and fumes as the fire rages outside. As the temperature inside the cabin increases it will eventually reach the flash point of the fumes which is much lower than the temperature needed to burn the actual materials inside the plane. Within a millisecond the fumes turn into a rolling boil of flames that race down the entire length of the cabin. Anyone who should be as unfortunate as to be standing in or just below those fumes when they ignite will be engulfed in that fire, scorching their lungs and causing death. Accident investigators have discovered countless fatalities in aviation accidents where the victims had no major physical injuries except that they were burned from the chest up from standing in the aisles, trapped as they were waiting to get out the front door when those fumes ignited.

How many of you know that during a loss of cabin pressure, when the oxygen masks drop down at your seat that you must first pull the pin out of the oxygen manifold in the ceiling before the flow of oxygen will start flowing to the mask? Almost all of you have heard this said during the pre-departure safety briefing: "fully extend the plastic tubing to start the flow of oxygen and place the mask around your mouth and nose." What passengers fail to understand is that fully extending that plastic tubing actually pulls a pin out of the oxygen delivery manifold at the top of the tube allowing oxygen to flow to the masks.

Above each section of seats there is a panel containing four oxygen masks, one for each seat and an extra for anyone carrying an infant in their lap. If the plane continually sent oxygen to every mask in the cabin the leaks would deplete the system and there would be nothing to breathe during an actual emergency. So airplane manufacturers installed those activation pins into each mask/manifold which must be pulled out before you'll get any oxygen even with the mask installed around your mouth and nose correctly. Some airlines, like Alaska or Allegiant actually put a picture of that pin on their safety briefing cards in the seat back pocket. Take a look the next time you're on a flight.

So what if you don't pull the pin? Probably not much other than you'll take a little nap and wake up with one heck of a headache! The plane will decompresses and the pilots will make an emergency descent down to 12,000'[13] where you no longer need the oxygen. Should you be involved in this type of situation and notice the person sitting next to you taking a nap, pull down on their plastic tubing!

But what if the masks don't drop at your seat? Just to cover this scenario aircraft manufacturers have installed a way to access the masks. During your next flight look up at the console above your seat and you'll see the panel containing the oxygen masks near the reading lights and flight attendant call button. On the panel will be a button or on older model aircraft a small hole. You can simply push the button to drop the panel down and access the masks, but if it's a hole you'll need to find a small object to insert into the hole in order to drop the panel in a manner similar to unlocking the interior doors of your house. The inside of a ball point pen or a paperclip usually work quite well if you can stay awake long enough to dig one out of your backpack and insert it into the hole. Please don't try testing the button before your next departure, it does work. Only use this technique during an actual emergency if the masks fail to deploy or you will delay the flight's departure for yourself and everyone else onboard as the crew has to call a mechanic out to reset the panel.

---

[13] Federal Aviation Regulations 121.333, 135.89 and 91.211

I believe the greatest thing airlines have done in the past decade that gives me a way to improve my own odds of surviving an accident is to allow me to go onto their website and choose my own seat! Most people choose their seat according to how close to their friends they can sit or how close to the front of the plane they can get in order to make a speedy exit. I choose my seat according to how close to an emergency exit I can get. All the seats are the same (except for the middle which nobody wants) so take a moment when choosing your seat and see where the exits are located, then make your best choice.

My first choice is always the exit row and even if I can't get into an exit row when booking my flight I always ask if one is available when checking in for the flight. The number one advantage for this is that I can be the first one out of the plane (if there is no fire on the other side of the door or window) if something goes wrong.

I brought this point up during one of our travel safety seminars in Yukon, Oklahoma many years ago to a wonderful group of people heading out on several overseas trips. After a minute or so an older lady toward the front raised her hand to ask me a question. She said "Isn't it dangerous going out an emergency exit?"

"Well not really," I answered. "The door just swings open after you rotate the lever, the exit windows weigh about 40 pounds and it just kind of falls inward when you pull the handle so you can just lay it on the seat or you can throw it out on the wing before you get out." I continued with my presentation and a few minutes later that same lady raised her hand again, "But where do you get the parachutes?" she asked. This comment took a couple of seconds for me to understand before her issue became fully clear.

"Ma'am (I'm from the south), you wait until the plane comes to a complete stop ON THE GROUND, then open the exit and get out." It turned out that this lady, in her 60's had never flown on an airplane before, had a huge fear of flying and was heading out of the country on her first flight going on an overseas vacation. Her learning curve that night was pretty much a straight line.

Questions like hers are really not that unusual. In my larger seminars with several hundred people in attendance, it's not unusual to find people who have never flown on an airplane before and it's very common to find a number of people who have never been out of the country or even out of the state they grew up in who are heading overseas for the first time. Hopefully this book will provide a lot of great information for you if you're in this category of travelers and you'll have a safe and wonderful trip!

The second advantage to sitting in an exit row is that exit rows have more leg room and at 6'2" I'll take all I can get; however, if it's a window exit where the plane has two window exit rows next to each other, I make sure that I choose the aft window exit row (closest to the rear of the aircraft) as the seats in the first row may not recline. Reclining the front row of seats can block access to the exit in the aft row during an emergency so these seats are modified to not recline. Depending on the length of the flight this can make for a very long flight sitting straight up and not being able to recline.

My second choice of seats will generally be an aisle seat depending on how close I can get to an emergency exit.

Within 5 or 6 rows of an exit I'll choose an aisle seat because I can get to the exit quickly before the route is blocked. Any farther away the window seat has some good advantages from an evacuation perspective. So why would a window seat have the advantage during an emergency evacuation when it's farther than 5 or 6 rows from the exit? Honestly, this seat provides an escape path to the nearest exit that most people never consider.

The next time you're on a commercial flight, watch what happens when the plane pulls up to the gate. Everyone jumps out of their seats, fills the aisle and nobody can move an inch. Now while everyone is standing in the aisle, take a look at the gap that is created over the window seats next to the fuselage between the top of the seat and the overhead luggage compartment. Granted, I would not take this route during a minor incident when everything seemed to be O.K., but if there were a fire outside or the cabin started filling up with smoke, I wouldn't hesitate to crawl right over the top of those window seats, to include the people still sitting in them, in order to get to an exit.

Before you pass judgment on this tactic there are a couple of things you should understand. First, if there is a fire outside the aircraft, or smoke inside, you have a very limited amount of time before everyone who is left inside that aircraft cabin will perish, so the sooner you get out the better. Second, just about everyone will forget about heading to the nearest exit and will make a bee-line for the forward entry door where they entered. They'll stack up in the aisle and if you are in the middle or toward the back of that line, there is a good chance that you won't get out.

People's reactions to emergencies generally fall into these categories:[14]

- 10-15%   react appropriately
- 75%   have to be told what to do
- 10-15%   react inappropriately

When it comes to crawling over the top of passengers you'll find that some people (10-15%) mentally shut down during an emergency or you've probably heard the term "frozen in fear." They are so overwhelmed with what is happening around them that their mental capacity to do anything is overloaded and they simply shut down. As you crawl over the top of these passengers (most likely putting a knee into their back, shoulder or head), yell and scream at them, telling them to get out of their seat and follow you. This action may shake them out of their mental stupor and save their life.

As you reach the nearest exit, check to ensure there is no fire outside by looking through the window, open the exit and then shout and scream as loud as you can for everyone to get out of their seats and follow you before you make your way to safety. Hopefully others will see the opening and follow you out. People following this escape option have saved hundreds of lives by getting other passengers to get out of their seats, out of that line of stacked-up passengers in the aisle and out of the aircraft.

To back up a bit, let's take a look at the question of when is it time to get out of your seat and head toward the exit. I bring this issue up as many survivable airline crashes have had numerous people killed because they got out of their seats before the accident was over. This may sound crazy

---

[14] Survival Phycology by Dr. John Leach, University of Lancaster

but it's true. In many crashes there is a huge initial impact, then the plane bounces back into the air for several seconds and everything seems to get smooth before the plane impacts the ground for a second time. Many fatalities have been caused by people who were in such a rush to get out that they reached down and released their seatbelts during that period of calmness between the initial impact and the second impact.

Many of you may remember the United Airlines flight 232 accident in Sioux Falls, SD. The plane had lost all hydraulic pressure after a catastrophic engine failure cut the hydraulic lines that controlled the steering. The pilots were using differential power settings between the two wing mounted engines and the pitch trim system in an attempt to steer the aircraft to the runway. The passengers had been briefed and prepared for the crash landing in advance. If you watch the video of the accident you can clearly see the aircraft hitting the runway, breaking into two main pieces and then bouncing back into the air for several seconds before crashing off the runway and into a corn field. Several passengers were found piled up into the forward bulkheads during the investigation, and investigators, trying to determine what caused their deaths, found the fingerprints for these passengers on the inside of the seatbelt buckle back at their seats. The only reason for their prints to be on the inside of the release mechanism would be from the passengers releasing the buckle themselves. So if you are ever unfortunate enough to be in an aircraft accident, wait until everything has come to a complete stop before you release your seatbelt and head for that emergency exit!

Flight 232 is also a good example of the statistics I used earlier. There were 295 people onboard that flight and if you look at the video of the accident which can be found on numerous internet video websites, you'd believe that everyone onboard that plane had been killed; however, there were 112 fatalities which means 183 people made it out alive[15]. Two thirds of the people who were involved in this horrific accident made it home.

Have you ever thought of counting the rows of seats between yours and the nearest emergency exit? As you board the plane and take your seat, take a look in front and behind you and count the number of seat rows to the nearest exit. Try to remember those numbers. Why? The flight attendant safety briefing usually says something like "in the event of an emergency, white lights lead to red lights and red lights lead to an exit" which sounds great except that during an actual emergency, when everyone is stacked as tight as sardines in that aisle trying to get to the front door, how many of you think you'll be able to see those little lights on the floor? And if the plane fills with smoke or if it's at night this will compound the issue even further; however, if you've remembered that the nearest exit is 6 rows forward, even if you can't see you can count the seatbacks as you make your way forward and then turn into the exit row while everyone else heads on past towards the front door.

You'd be amazed at the number of people who were sitting right next to an exit window during an emergency, got out of their seat and headed to the front door! It's human nature to head out where you came in. Should you ever find yourself in an airline evacuation, you need to go to the *"nearest"* exit, open it and get as many people to follow you out of that exit as possible.

---

[15] www.ntsb.gov/investigations/AccidentReports/Pages/AAR9006.aspx

The number two cause of deaths during airline accidents from people who survive the impact but die before getting out of the plane is from flail or impact injuries. Impact injuries come from flying debris. The majority of these come from items in the overhead storage bins. The latches on many of these bins will fail during an accident and everything inside those bins will become flying missiles. With the latest trend in aviation being to charge a fee to check every piece of luggage, people these days are packing everything they have into a carry-on bag and placing it in the overhead bin. Some of these bags weigh as much as 70 pounds and when flying through the air at untold speeds become very dangerous and deadly objects.

Flail injuries are those caused when your arms and legs are flying around during the crash. If you've ever watched crash test dummies you've surely noticed their extremities flailing about. If you are slammed forward during an aircraft accident and break both of your forearms on the seat in front of you, think about how difficult it would be to unbuckle your seatbelt with your elbows! Airline accident investigators have found many people who died from smoke inhalation sitting in their seats because they could not unlatch their seatbelt due to flail injuries. So I want to provide you with a few very simple practices that you can employ when flying that may prevent these injuries from happening.

First and foremost, you should adopt a proper takeoff and landing sitting position. This may sound silly but it's not and honestly nobody except you will even notice. Just before takeoff (as the plane turns onto the runway and the power on the engines starts to increase) or just before landing (you hear the landing gear being extended or you can see outside the window and are approaching the ground) sit up straight, slide your backside as far back in the seat as you possibly can and snug your seatbelt up as tight as it will go. Now place your feet flat on the floor, don't have them underneath the seat in front of you and either cross your arms across your chest or place your hands/fingers under your legs between your legs and the arm rest of your seat. This is the seated position flight attendants are supposed to be in for every takeoff and landing. On takeoff, as soon as the landing gear is raised, or on landing, as soon as the plane starts to pull off the runway you can resume a comfortable, relaxed sitting position.

Why? First, by crossing your arms or sitting on your hands, you will keep them in place should the plane have an unexpected accident (wind shear, another plane pulling out onto the runway, or a catastrophic engine failure.) By sitting in this position you won't slam your arms into the seat in front of you, breaking your forearms and you'll stay tightly seated in your seat.

I assume this posture for every takeoff and landing and I do it so effortlessly that I've only had one person ever notice. Recently I was on my way back from Miami and just prior to touchdown I went through this little procedure of tightening my seatbelt and crossing my arms when I looked across the aisle and noticed the man sitting across from me doing the exact same thing. He kindly smiled and nodded at me in a manner to say "well done, we both know how to travel safely." I nodded back and had a big smile across my face that couldn't be held back. The only other person who will ever notice your actions will be another well-educated traveler. In the unlikelihood that something goes wrong during takeoff or landing, which is the most dangerous part of your flight, your chances of surviving that accident will have just gone up by simply adjusting how you sit.

The second part of this procedure is to duck if anything feels or sounds wrong. If there is a sudden drop, if the captain suddenly slams on the breaks after touch down, or any number of things that feel out of the norm, duck your head as low as possible to avoid any flying debris that may come out of those overhead bins. It doesn't even take an accident for the overhead bins to fail. Many will pop open during nothing more than a hard landing.

Numerous people have been seriously injured by carry-on bags when their plane experienced a hard landing. These injuries were not the result of an accident. The plane may have encountered a wind shear just before touching down or possibly caught a little unexpected turbulence from a plane that previously landed which caused their flight to hit the runway harder than usual. Anyone who has traveled much has experienced these types of landings as they are not uncommon. A hard landing can cause the latch on one of the overhead bins to fail and open. If the plane jerks to one side it can cause a 50+ pound carry-on bag to dislodge from the bin and come flying out, striking a passenger with serious force resulting in major injuries.

I stated that part of this takeoff or landing posture was to place your feet on the floor and not underneath the seat in front of you. This is especially important during landings! Have you ever noticed that strange bend in the bottom legs on airline seats? Let me tell you why they are built that way.

The FAA runs a facility at their campus in Oklahoma City called CAMI. It stands for Civil Aerospace Medical

Institute.[16] One section at CAMI is dedicated to testing airline equipment to help improve safety. What accident investigators found many years ago in several crashes and some even in very hard landings was that people who were otherwise uninjured had broken backs from the initial impact. That bend in the seat legs was tested at CAMI and is designed to fail, crushing downward just prior to the force that it takes to break the average person's back. This seat modification has saved a lot of people from breaking their spine but this design also causes a secondary problem.

During a number of fatal airline accidents where the investigators went in afterward to look at the deceased victims in order to determine why or how they died, they found perfectly healthy people sitting dead in their seats from smoke inhalation because their feet were pinned under the seat in front of them. The next time you fly, take a look at how people are seated, especially young people who assume that relaxed, laid-out posture with their legs stretched out as far as possible under the seat in front of them. This posture is fine if you're comfortable that way "except" during takeoffs and landings! In the unlikely event of an airline accident, by simply placing your feet flat on the floor in front of your seat and not underneath the seat in front of you, you will avoid this potential hazard.

Most of what I am asking you to do in this book is to simply change a few habits such as how you dress, sit in a seat or watch where you go. These simple changes can greatly reduce the odds of having anything go wrong or greatly improve your odds of surviving if it does.

If you are involved in an accident and make it out of the plane safely, never go back for anything. Earlier I

---

[16] www.faa.gov/about/office_org/headquarters_offices/avs/offices/aam/cami/

discussed the flash fires that can happen when the smoke and fumes ignite inside an aircraft cabin. You don't want to be inside the aircraft if that happens. Pull, help and coax anyone you can to get out of the plane with you; however, once you are outside move at least 300 yards away from the wreckage, preferably to the side of the flight path to a place of safety and stay there. Do not go back in!

I specifically listed the types of clothing you should wear when flying on a plane, blue jeans, cotton shirt and lace-up shoes being the best all-around option, and the types of clothing you should not wear. Here is why I recommend this simple dress code. First of all it's quite comfortable but more importantly it provides a significant amount of protection should you be involved in an accident. Next to fire retardant Nomex, which I doubt anyone will be wearing, cotton provides a great deal of protection from fires and sharp objects. Unlike nylon which I discussed earlier, cotton will char rather than burn and it won't melt into your skin like synthetics do.

I'd like to point out a couple of examples of airline accidents that have happened during overseas trips:

First is the August 25, 2008, crash that happened 60 miles east of Guatemala City.[17] The commuter flight from Aurora to El Estor included 10 college students who were on an end of summer trip with Choice Humanitarian Missions out of Utah. The small C208 Caravan commuter plane struck a tree and crashed into a field around 9:45 a.m. Eight of the American students on the trip were killed in the accident. When you look at the pictures from the event you have to wonder how many might have survived had they been wearing proper clothing or sitting in a protective

---

[17] www.newrichmond-news.com/content/father-and-son-amery-die-guatemalan-air-crash

position. The wreckage was extensive with a great deal of shredded metal and fire damage but parts of the plane were survivable. When you view the pictures of the survivors and victims, you'll notice that they were all wearing shorts, sandals or flip flops and many with nylon or some other type of synthetic shirt. It was reported that most of the victims died from burns and smoke inhalation. These injuries came after the crash and may have been prevented by employing the simple techniques that I have recommended in this chapter.

Another example on how to survive an airline accident happened with the Mosier family. The Mosiers were working in Tanzania when they decided to make a trip over to the Congo to see their son who was starting a new project. On April 15, 2008, during what seemed like a normal takeoff, one of the engines developed an uncontrollable fire. The pilot elected to abort the takeoff too late and the plane skidded off the end of the runway and into a crowded market. With the exception of the pilots, all of the passengers most likely survived the initial crash.

Of the 4 members of the family, the daughter found herself outside the aircraft and unharmed while Mr. Mosier, his wife and son were trapped inside. They first tried to make their way to the front of the plane (heading toward the forward entry door like everyone else does) but could not get there. Their efforts to make it to the back of the plane were blocked by wreckage and fire. Mr. Mosier found a crack in the fuselage and with his hands made the opening big enough for the remaining family members to make it out. This is the type of survival spirit that every passenger should have: "Whatever it takes, I will get out of here and I will survive." The Mosiers escaped with just minor cuts and burns while 47 others did not make it out.[18]

The next airline issue discussed involves dealing with problem passengers. Anyone who has traveled very much has seen other passengers get out of control during the flight. Some people are set off by delays or lack of food, but the most common trigger is too much alcohol. Many good people want to just jump up and assist the crew when a passenger gets out of hand and sometimes this is necessary; however, you need to wait a moment and consider what could happen before you react.

The general rule of thumb is that you should not assist a crewmember with a problem passenger unless they specifically ask for help. They are trained to ask for assistance if they need it and if/when they do, give them all you can. Crewmembers are trained to handle problem passengers and it is part of their job but they will ask for help if they need it.

The other issue to consider is that there very well may be law enforcement officers onboard your flight. Federal Air Marshalls and Law Enforcement Officers know that one tactic utilized by terrorist organizations is to have one member of their terrorist team cause a diversionary problem to draw out any police officers that may be on board. When law enforcement officers make themselves known, the other members of the terror group will attack the law enforcement officers and disable them first before taking control of the aircraft. For this reason, if you were to get up to help before a crewmember specifically asks for assistance you could possibly get arrested by an Air Marshall or Police Officer thinking that you might be part

---

[18] www.usatoday30.usatoday.com/news/world/2008-04-15-2827678812_x.htm

of a terrorist plot. The best thing to do is to stay seated, pay attention to what is happening so that you can be a good witness and possibly "offer" your assistance if given the opportunity.

A problem passenger onboard an aircraft is extremely different from a hijacking situation and requires different actions. The first thing to do in any hijacking situation is to ask yourself, "What type of hijacking is this?"

Hijackings are basically broken down into two categories. First is the criminal hijacking. These people have a demand. They want money, a prisoner exchange or simply to be taken to another country other than the intended destination. Criminal hijackings, although they may take a while to conclude, usually end with the safe return of the plane and passengers. For these, it's best to simply sit quietly, try not to make eye contact and be the most cooperative passenger you can be.

A terrorist hijacking is a much different situation. They usually start with the words "Allah Akbar," meaning God is the greatest and nothing can be greater than God. Not a bad philosophy except that they are using it in a holy war context meaning that God is directing them to take over that airplane and kill as many of the infidels as possible in the process, both in the plane and on the ground! They don't demand anything; they only want control of that plane in order to use it as a weapon. The rules for passengers in a terrorist hijacking are quite different than they are for a criminal hijacking. There basically are none!

My recommendation is to get your wits about you and wait no more than 20 to 30 seconds. If Federal Air Marshalls (FAMs) are onboard your flight, you'll know it within that timeframe. If FAMs start to take action get down as low as possible and out of the line of fire! It will be one of the most violent acts you've ever been near and most likely there will be collateral damage to innocent victims.

If after 20 to 30 seconds nothing is happening to stop the terrorist actions, I recommend that if you are physically able, do whatever you can to stop their attempts to take control of the aircraft. If this means that several passengers die in the process then that's a favorable outcome. Harsh reality? No! You have to realize that if the terrorists are able to take over that plane, EVERYONE onboard, every single passenger and crewmember will die. It's just a matter of where the impact is going to take place. So if you were to die in the process of trying to protect the other 150 passengers onboard and succeed then you've accomplished a great service to the survivors. If you are not successful then you may arrive at the pearly gates a few minutes prior to everyone else.

I've had many people comment to me that this is considered murder. It is not. The actions of the terrorist would be murder. They came onboard that flight with the specific intent to kill everyone onboard including as many people on the ground as possible. That is murder. If you killed any of the terrorists in the act of trying to protect the other passengers onboard, then that is simply an unfortunate circumstance from an act of self-defense.

One way to look at the difference is to consider your actions after the event. Should you be successful and the terrorists were to die, treat your wounds and then pray for their souls; however, if they were to live, treat your wounds, secure the terrorists so they can't hurt anyone and then spend the rest of the flight before you land preaching to them the forgiveness of their sins and the love of our savior Jesus Christ. It will be a concept that they cannot comprehend. They would expect for you to finish them off if they failed, not to forgive them and pray for them. You'll blow their minds!

When I first went into law enforcement I struggled a little bit with this moral concept, so I turned to my Bible and asked God to show me what I needed to know. I literally opened my Bible to the following passages. It's the section in the New Testament where the high priest's slave and the Roman soldiers are coming to seize Jesus and take him into custody before going to the cross. I first opened the pages to Luke 22:38 - "Lord, look, here are two swords" and Jesus said to them, "It is enough." I then opened the pages again to Luke 22:49 – And when those who were around Him saw what was going to happen, they said, "Lord, shall we strike with the sword?"

I thought about these verses for a while and, being a long time law enforcement officer, I realized the following facts. In the days of Jesus just about everyone carried a small dagger style of knife. It was used for everyday chores from eating to field work, but carrying a sword was like someone today carrying a Smith and Wesson 357 pistol. In those days very few people carried swords other than soldiers (the police of that time), robbers or possibly people who provided personal protection to some affluent person. I suddenly saw Jesus's disciples in a whole new light. They were not only followers of His teachings but were also his body guards (maybe that's why he picked big strong professional fishermen).

I opened my Bible again and this time went straight to John 18:10 – Simon Peter, therefore having a sword, drew it and struck the high priest's slave and cut off his right ear. Jesus therefore said to Peter, "Put the sword into the sheath."

Now if you think about that action, you don't just reach up and cut off someone's ear. I believe that Peter was swinging at the slave's head with the intent of separating it from his shoulders, the high priest's slave ducked and the blade of the sword struck the bony park of his skull, sliding down and taking off his ear. Peter was willing to kill the high priest's slave if necessary to protect our Lord Jesus.

So how does this apply to handling our airline terrorist situation? Each person must make his or her own decision about what to do during a crisis situation like this. My personal belief as a law enforcement officer is that if I end up killing someone during the course of my actions to protect a plane load of wonderful Christians heading out to serve our Lord on a mission trip, when I arrive at the pearly gates Peter, having been the one who tried to take the head off the high priests slave to protect our Lord, will understand my actions. I use this same philosophy with any security issue where I may have to defend myself or others in my party.

6

Hotel Safety and Security

After one of the longest days of your life, traveling from the US to wherever your overseas trip takes you, most people walk into their hotel room, throw their bags down on the floor, hit the bed and pass out. But before you take that well deserved rest there are a few basic steps you should take in order to keep yourself safe and secure.

If you are traveling with a number of people everyone in the group should exchange basic personal information with everyone else in the party. In the appendix at the back of this book I have included a sample of specific items that need to be included in your emergency action plan. That information needs to be shared with and carried by each person in your traveling group. If something happened to you would everyone else know who to call or what to do? Do you have any medical issues like high blood pressure, diabetes or heart trouble? These are not issues that should be kept hidden from your traveling companions. If you carry insulin or nitroglycerin in your jacket pocket, don't be embarrassed to let your companions know that you have it and where it's located. Hopefully it never happens but if for some reason you go down during your trip and are unable to communicate, you want to make sure that your traveling companions know where it is and what to do.

Hotels house people who are away from home, generally carrying large amounts of money (as compared to the average citizen) and the rooms have minimal security. How many keys do you think have been issued that will open your door? There are only a limited number of key cuts or electronic bar codes that are programmed into those plastic keys, not to mention all the master keys issued to employees and the numerous ways to simply bypass the door locks all together. Even here in the US, hotel rooms have a number of hidden dangers that most people never consider. Depending on what part of the world you are in, your hotel may very well be one of the most dangerous places you'll visit. These threats come not only from other humans but from disasters such as a major fire. Consider for a moment what a hotel really is, a facility holding thousands of sleeping people who are unfamiliar with their surroundings, confined in a multi-story building with few escape routes. This view is not meant to instill fear when staying in hotels but simply to make you aware of the hidden dangers that most people never consider. There are, however, a few simple steps that you can take which can greatly reduce or even eliminate the risk of something bad happening to you at your hotel.

In addition to the rare but devastating major fire event, every day people are robbed, attacked and sexually assaulted in major hotels in every large city of the world. These facts are not widely publicized by hotel chains or travel agents because it would be detrimental to their business which is tied so closely to tourism and commerce. In this chapter I'll discuss the dangers hotels pose along with some very simple procedures you can employ in order to greatly improve the odds that you won't become a victim and will be able to survive any disaster that may arise.

Let's start by taking a look at how you should choose your accommodations and, just like selecting your airline seat, make a safety related room choice. Around the world lodging is usually broken down into two forms, hotels and motels. (Lodges, hostels and other types of lodging will fall into one of these categories.) Hotels are categorized by a lack of outside access. To reach a hotel room one must enter the building first and walk down a hallway to reach his or her room. Motels on the other hand provide outside access directly to the room. You are able to drive up to or walk up to your room at a motel without having to go inside the building and past the front desk clerk. Some lodging will have a combination of both types of room access.

By far, the hotel is a safer choice from a security standpoint. People who are looking for someone to rob or sexually assault would prefer not to walk past the front desk where they can be seen and possibly recognized. When you have a choice, choose a hotel. When you stay at a location that has both types of access, ask for a room that only has access into a corridor, not direct access from outside.

The biggest safety threat in hotels comes from fires. These events are few and far between; however, when fires do happen in multi-story hotels they can result in a huge loss of life due simply to the fact that you may have thousands of people staying in a single building with very limited escape routes. The second most serious security issue is from being attacked, robbed or sexually assaulted which can happen at either of these types of accommodations. This happens much more frequently than you would think, so here are a number of very simple practices that you can employ to help keep yourself safe from both of these threats.

One of the first things I do when checking into a hotel, if they don't give it to me, is to ask if they have a room available between the 2nd and the 6th floors. This may seem odd to you the first time you do it, but just about everyone working at the check-in desk at a hotel will know exactly why you are asking.

The first floor is not preferred from a security standpoint. Criminals looking for a victim will attempt to find one on the first floor if possible. They don't want to be trapped several floors up after committing their crime which would require them to either take the stairs or elevator down to an exit in order to escape. Gaining entry onto the ground floor without walking past the front desk is as easy as waiting for a guest to open the door at the end of the hall and letting you in. Many times the guest will even hold the door open for the criminals as they walk into the hotel. Many of us are probably guilty of it, walking out the door at the end of the hall, which requires a key to open from the outside, only to find someone walking in carrying luggage. So being the wonderfully nice people that we are, we hold the door open for them. Please let this be the last time you do that! Require anyone who is trying to get inside any entrance other than the front door to use their room key to open the door to ensure the key they have actually works. Some of the criminals are very professional and will have an old key they picked up in the parking lot or trash bin in their hand. They stand near the door with an empty bag and wait for someone to exit the building before they walk right in while you hold the door for them.

Why would you not want to be above the 6th floor? The answer boils down to a basic mechanical issue. The ladder on a fire truck can't reach above the 6th floor so if you are staying in a room above the 6th floor in a hotel and have a fire in a lower floor, there is no way to escape but to walk down the stairs through the smoke and flames (yes, it has happened.)

What should you do during check-in at the hotel and the clerk says they are completely full and don't have a room located between the 2nd and 6th floor? You take the room you're given and pay a little more attention to items such as the location of the stairwells and of course pay close attention to any fire alarms. Should the alarm sound you'll need to take quick, positive actions, get up and get out.

This 2nd to 6th floor issue is why most new hotels are being built with only 3 to 6 stories. There have been so many lawsuits over loss of life during fires in those huge sky rise hotels that large hotel chains have found it cheaper to purchase multiple pieces of property and build multiple buildings within the same general location. That is why you see hotel chains like Hilton or Marriott building hotels under different brand names such as a Hilton, Hilton Garden Inn, Hampton Inn and Homewood Suites right next to each other. The same is true with brands such as Marriott with the Residence Inn and Spring Hill Suites, etc. Financially they want to accommodate the same number of guest but don't want the liability issue with the mega-story building. Where land is at a premium, as in downtown Chicago or New York City, they don't have this option so you'll still see the mega hotels being built.

Victims of crimes in hotels are often chosen by the criminals in the lobby or at the front desk. Believe it or not it doesn't take a law degree to get hired to work the front counter or as a doorman at a hotel. Often these people will be paid to provide information about potential targets such as the type of person along with their room number. Women staying by themselves are usually the primary choice of criminals due to their size and inability to fight back, with wealthy business men being second.

When planning your security-related practices at your hotel start by not broadcasting your intentions in the lobby for everyone to hear. How many times have you traveled with someone who stood in the lobby announcing to everyone within ear shot that everyone in your group is about to leave all of their money and valuables unattended in their rooms for the next two hours? You're probably thinking never, but if you've travelled very often with a group of people you're probably guilty of it.

The scene usually goes something like this. Someone will announce quite loudly, "Ok guys, let's go upstairs, drop our bags and meet back down here in 15 minutes to go get dinner." Sound familiar? Think about this statement from a criminal's perspective. Anyone listening now knows that in 15 minutes they have at least an hour to break into your room and take everything of value that you've brought with you! That type of information needs to be either discussed in the taxi before you arrive at the hotel or held private until you have left the lobby and are in the safe confines of the elevator heading up to your room or in the hallway where nobody else will hear it.

Checking into your hotel you'll find business cards located on the counter next to the check-in desk at just about every hotel around the world. Pick up one of those business cards and place it in your wallet or purse. If they have business cards written in both English and the local language, grab one of each. These cards carry some valuable information that you may find quite useful during your stay. It contains the name of the hotel, the address and phone number written in the local language which can be shown to a policeman or taxi driver who may not speak English.

For the females reading this book please pay attention to this next security practice. Women staying in hotel rooms by themselves or even those staying with another female traveling companion are the number one targets of criminals. They have a higher statistical chance of being robbed or sexually assaulted than men traveling by themselves or with their wives. To combat this issue, there is a very simple tactic that people traveling together can employ that can help protect the women against attacks.

If you are traveling with a group of people that include males and females, once you leave the hotel lobby area, like in the elevator or when you reach your room floor, have the women exchange room keys with the men. That way, at 2 o'clock in the morning when someone knocks on the woman's hotel room door hoping that she'll just open it without first looking through the peep hole to see who it is, a heavy male voice will ask, "Who is it and what do you want?" The criminal is expecting a female voice and that simple act of switching rooms will shock the criminal who will walk away, preventing this type of attack against women staying by themselves. For you men, if this happens and you hear the person on the other side of the door seem shocked, state that they must have the wrong room and then leave. Congratulations! You have just prevented an attempted robbery or sexual assault that was directed at one of your female traveling companions. My number one rule on hotel safety is that you never open the door unless you know for sure who is there. If for any reason you are concerned about the person on the other side, keep the door closed, call the front desk and ask for assistance.

There is another very serious safety concern when using this key swapping tactic. This issue only applies to married people not traveling with their spouses. This security threat may be more detrimental to your personal safety than any other I'll present so please pay attention! Make sure you tell your spouse, before you leave home, that you may be doing this! When little Johnny can't sleep because Daddy's gone and the wife calls the hotel, asks to be connected to Mr. Webb's room and some sweet-sounding woman answers the phone, it may result in a serious threat to your personal safety and security (if not your life) when you arrive back home! Enough said.

Make your way from the hotel lobby to your room, take a moment in route and locate the nearest exit. Overseas travelers often find themselves staying in big, beautiful old hotels that were built when liability law suits were not an issue. Simply put, as beautiful as these hotels are and as much as I enjoy staying in them, they do pose the greatest risks to your personal safety and security.

The fire codes when these buildings were constructed were nowhere close to the building codes of today. Many of these older hotels were built with lots of twists and turns in the hallway layout which may make locating the nearest exit difficult. Sometimes the nearest exit can be down the hall, turn left, then right and around the corner to the stairwell. If this is the case, take that hotel business card you picked up at the front desk and draw a little map on the back of it. Should you need to get out in a hurry take the card, look at the map and go!

Additionally, when you walk into your room, take a moment to look out the window and get your bearings. Often you'll think you should be facing the back side of the hotel only to find that your window is facing the front. Check to see if the windows or sliding doors open. Try them and find out. Some may open, some may only partially open and some may be mechanically locked shut. Look to see if there is a fire-escape outside. Is there a roof on a lower floor below your window that could be used to escape if needed? This bearing check only takes a few seconds and is not to be dwelt on. Once you know what you have to work with or deal with, file the information away in the back of your mind and continue on with unpacking and enjoying your stay. It's the same simple tactic as counting the rows to the nearest exit in the airplane.

One of the safety procedures I've adopted in hotels is to always place my room key and wallet on the corner of the nearest object to the exit, usually the dresser, with my shoes placed on the floor directly below them. In the event that I need to make a hasty retreat from the room in the dark I have everything I need right where I need it: the key to my room in order to get back in, my wallet (or purse for you ladies) with money and identification, and shoes to protect my feet. I'll never have to hunt for these items if I'm in a hurry to get out. I also carry a very small LED flashlight that I usually keep next to the bed. These small lights, about the size of a quarter, offer years of battery life and enough illumination to see how to get around the room, down the hall and out of the building should all power sources be lost.

To assist with moving around during a power outage I don't sleep in total darkness. Leave the curtains open just enough to allow enough outside ambient light into the room that you can locate your key, wallet, shoes and see where you need to go. It doesn't take much and most hotel rooms leak that amount of light into the room without any adjustment to the curtains. At home you can probably wake up in the middle of the night, walk over and place your hand directly on the door knob virtually every time without even opening your eyes. It's called muscle memory, you've done it thousands of times; however, in an unfamiliar hotel room when you wake up smelling smoke with the alarm blaring overhead and the electricity out, locating your personal items and finding that door knob isn't quite as easy.

Another recommendation is to both lock and block your doors and windows. Use all of the locks, deadbolts and chains provided by the hotel but as a professional who's taught lock-picking skills to countless law enforcement officers, a hotel room door, even without a key, can be opened in a matter of seconds without making a sound using something as simple as a length of bendable metal rod and a piece of string. For this reason, in addition to locking the door, I block it using a small, light-weight plastic wedge. Their weight is negligible, they are easy to pack and even if someone is able to unlock your door they can't open it.

For the past decade I've carried a ten dollar item called the Wedgeit. It's a specially designed plastic wedge originally made for law enforcement officers that prevents people from shutting a door on them during search warrants. This device has recently been adopted by a number of cleaning and service companies to keep the doors open when the maids are inside cleaning. Many hotels provide their maids with Wedgeits so that they can block the doors open, preventing unwanted persons from coming in and shutting the door, trapping them inside the room (maids have been sexually assaulted in hotels too.) You can use this Wedgeit to do the opposite and block your hotel room door shut.

Placing a Wedgeit under your hotel room door will prevent anyone from *opening* your door even if they have a key.

What actions do you normally take when you wake up at 2 a.m. with the hotel alarm going off? If you're like most people you'll get up, look out into the hallway only to see a dozen other people looking up and down the hall, too. If you don't smell smoke or see people running for the exits, most people will ignore the alarm and go back to bed. Please don't do this! Take a few minutes to do more of an investigation and check to see if there may actually be a fire, certainly more than just looking down the hall. Call the front desk and ask the operator if this is a false alarm. Open the window and look around to see if you can smell or see smoke or maybe hear fire trucks coming your way. If you get any indication that there might actually be a fire, gather your belongings and head for the stairs.

If the desk clerk tells you that it is a false alarm and will be turned off within a minute or two then relax and see if that actually happens. If the alarm does not go off within just a minute or two or if nobody answers the front desk phone, pick up your wallet, room key, put on your shoes and take a walk down the stairs and go outside. What's the worse that will happen? If it actually was a false alarm you'll lose a half hour of sleep and might be a little tired the next day; however, if it was not a false alarm, this 30 minutes may save your life!

Most people believe that if they walk out into the hallway and don't *smell* any smoke it must be a false alarm and they go back to bed. The problem with this action is that many, if not most of the old hotels placed their restaurants on the top floor where they get a great view of the city. Where do most hotel fires start? In the kitchen, of course, and what

99

does smoke do? It rises, so if the fire is on the roof or on one of the floors above you, you won't smell the smoke when looking out into the hallway. When you look at statistics on the most devastating hotel fires in history, most of them started with a fire on the roof. What happens is the alarm goes off, everyone looks out into the hallway and doesn't see or smell anything and everyone goes back to bed, covers their head with a pillow so they don't have to listen to that darn siren and tries to go back to sleep. This happens as the fire begins to engulf the entire upstairs until the structure of the floor weakens, starts to buckle and eventually collapses on the floors below. Well, you can figure out the rest of the story with those sleeping guests who ignored the alarm and didn't lose that precious 30 minutes of sleep thinking that this was probably a false alarm. The next time you enter a newer hotel notice that the restaurant has been built on the ground floor or in an older hotel has been relocated to the ground floor and now you know why.

What if you look out into the hallway and do smell smoke? That indicates that the fire is either below you, on your floor or very close above. Now it's time to get out quickly; however, if you can smell the smoke I want you to delay your exit for about 20 seconds. Take this time to walk into the bathroom, grab a towel, place it under the faucet in the bath tub, turn on the water, get it wet and take that wet towel with you. Do you remember watching people escaping the World Trade Center buildings before they collapsed? If you'll think back to that scene most of those people had a black ring of soot around their mouth and nose. This was caused by the smoke and soot they had to walk through as they made their way down the stairs adhering to the moisture in their breath causing it to cling to their face. What you saw on the outside was also attached to their lungs on the inside. The media has run numerous stories about police officers and firefighters who survived the tower collapse only to suffer horrendous physical disabilities caused by those toxic fumes and smoke. What the news doesn't talk about are all the civilians who made it out of the buildings that also suffered those devastating lung injuries.

You never want to take an elevator during a fire evacuation. The fire could be raging inside the elevator shaft which can engulf the elevator itself as you transit down to the ground floor with no way to escape. You should always take the stairs! Should you be walking down the stairs and encounter a cloud of smoke and fumes, use that wet towel as a filter to breathe through. That same wet towel can be used as a fire shield in the event that you come across a wall of flames and have no choice but to run through it in order to escape. The extra 20 seconds it took to obtain that one simple item, a wet towel, can literally save your life.

In addition to the threats in your hotel room, many of the robberies and sexual assaults that have taken place in hotels have occurred in the elevators. For years I have been teaching people that if you are traveling alone or in a very small group and a single male or small group of young men (between the ages of 18-35) are standing in the elevator when the door opens, act like you forgot something, turn around and walk back toward your room until the door shuts. Once the elevator has started moving go back and push the button for the next elevator to stop.

If you think about what an elevator is, other than a means to transit floors without over exerting yourself, it is a small, enclosed, soundproof chamber that criminals have been known to utilize to locate and trap their victims. This is accomplished by simply riding up and down in the elevator until their victim steps inside and the doors close.

In Gavin De Becker's book, *The Gift of Fear*,[19] he uses an excellent example of what can happen in a hotel elevator. De Becker chronicles the story of a woman who was brutally sexually assaulted in an elevator. I'll take a little creative licensing with his story to get the point across.

Rebecca is on a business trip which encountered a few delays. Her flight was late and she had to run through the airport terminal in order to make her connection. Arriving late at her destination she picks up her luggage and grabs the first taxi she finds to the hotel. Checking in and getting settled into her room Rebecca suddenly realizes that she hasn't had the opportunity to eat all day, it's now 9 p.m. and she is really hungry, so Rebecca decides to go down to the restaurant in the hotel lobby for a bite. Rebecca leaves her room, walks down the hallway and pushes the button for the elevator. As the elevator door opens she notices a single man standing in the back of the elevator. Her statements during the investigation with police are as follows:

"When the elevator door opened I saw a man inside. I'm not usually afraid," she said. "Maybe it was the late hour, his size or the way he looked at me but for some reason I had just a moment of apprehension." This was Rebecca's natural intuition kicking in letting her know that something was wrong! "But he seemed like such a nice man. I'm not going to live like that," she said to herself. "I'm not going to insult this guy by letting the door close in his face.

---

[19] The Gift of Fear by Gavin de'Becker

When the fear didn't pass I told myself, 'I'm not going to be so silly' so I got into the elevator."

It was there that Rebecca's life changed forever. Rebecca stepped into that elevator, the door closed and she was brutally raped.

So let me ask you a question about Rebecca's actions. Which is sillier? Letting the elevator door shut and waiting a minute or two for the next elevator to arrive, or getting into a soundproof, steel chamber with a stranger she was already afraid of? It sounds so simple in hind sight. Her intuition was there, she was already weary of this guy, so why did she get in? Believe it or not most of us would probably get into that elevator without a second thought. Hopefully you won't from this day forward.

Take this safety philosophy past just the elevators! You need to incorporate this philosophy into any situation where your intuition has kicked in and it is trying to tell you that something is wrong!

Intuition occurs when your subconscious brain is operating at warp speed and recognizes some sort of danger even though your conscious mind doesn't recognize it. That sudden feeling that something is wrong happens when your mind picks up cues, whether visual, audible, a smell or any number of different inputs that tell your brain that there is danger and it's trying to let you know that something is wrong. When these sudden intuitive feelings take place, you should take one of two courses of action:

> a) Take just a moment to absorb your surroundings to determine the source of the danger, or

b) Take the safer approach of just trusting your intuition, turning toward the nearest route to safety and start moving!

Hindsight being 20/20, what could or better yet, what should Rebecca have done when that elevator door opened and she saw a man standing inside and suddenly felt that rush of intuition? One of the easiest things to do in this situation would be to pretend you forgot something, place your hand on your pocket and say. "Ah, I forgot my wallet," then simply turn around and walk back toward your room until the elevator door closes. Then you can either go back and press the elevator button and wait for the next one to arrive or take the stairs.

One note of caution, if the next time the elevator door opens and that same guy is standing inside, turn around, run to your room and call hotel security! This may be a criminal trolling inside the elevator waiting for his next victim to step inside.

After getting their key, most weary travelers walk in their room, throw their bags on the floor and either hit the bed, check their email or turn on the TV to relax. Even through you may be dead tired please take a few extra seconds to find the nearest exit, lock and block your door, look out the window to get your bearings, place your to-go items (wallet, key and shoes) next to the exit and then settle down to relax. These simple security practices only take a few seconds and can pay huge dividends should the unlikely security event happen before the wake-up alarm goes off the next morning.

When you are ready to leave your room for the day make sure that you've secured your valuables and travel documents. When it comes to securing these items I do use the in-room safes with the addition of one simple check before I leave my items inside, which has to do with the factory settings on the safe. What if, during a long day away from the hotel you were to forget the security code you entered into the in-room safe? Actually, I'm not that worried about forgetting the code because the hotel manager has a master code that will override anything you put in, but it's this master code that I'm concerned with. Most hotel safe manufacturers set the original master code at 0000 when the units are shipped from the factory. When the hotel installs the safe they are supposed to change the original master code to something else; however, a very large percentage of hotels never change this code! So before I leave my money, valuables and travel documents in the hotel safe, I give it the 0000 test.

Close the door on the safe and enter your favorite security code. Let's use 3456 as an example. When you enter your personal security code the door to the safe should lock. Now that the safe is secure with your personal code, enter the original default code of 0000 and see if it opens. If not then the master code has been changed and it's fairly unlikely that a maid or anyone other than the hotel manager will know the current master code. However, if you enter 0000 and the safe opens, look for another option for your belongings.

For this I do the same as I would if my hotel room didn't have an in-room safe, go to the front desk and ask for a safety deposit box. Most domestic and just about every international hotel has safety deposit boxes for their guests to use. These boxes are either free or available for a very nominal fee. If the room does not have a safe or if the manufacturer's default code hasn't been changed I'll take my valuables downstairs and ask for one of these safety deposit boxes before leaving the hotel for the day.

Another security measure I use when leaving my room is to turn the TV on with the volume turned up just loud enough to be heard outside the door (but not so loud that it bothers my neighbors.) I want anyone who might have an extra key to my room, intent on coming in while I'm gone to steal my belongings, to think that someone else might still be in the room even though they saw me leave. It's a tactic that actually works fairly well. The hotel maid will knock on the door and come in anyway if nobody answers, but a criminal might not.

There is one last issue I'd like to address regarding hotel safety before I move on to other topics. Incorporating this one simple tactic will save more people from robberies and sexual assaults than any other advice I've discussed so far. It is simply to NEVER open the door when somebody knocks on it without first looking to see who it is! This sounds so simple but at times it might not be, especially when you are expecting someone to come over.

The most common tactic utilized by assailants to gain access to you and your belongings is to simply knock on the door in hopes that the unsuspecting guest inside will simply walk over and open the door without thinking about who is on the other side. This is usually followed by the assailant either kicking the door into their face or shoving them back into the room and closing the door behind them. Quite often this will happen in the early hours of the morning when guests have been asleep, not paying attention and there are no other witnesses.

If someone knocks on your door, "DO NOT OPEN IT!!" Take a moment to look through the peep hole, see who is on the other side and ask what they want. If it's a friend or a co-worker that you were expecting, check and make sure that is actually who is at the door and that somebody you don't know is standing behind them before you open the door (we'll cover this issue in a minute).

Not opening the door when someone knocks on it would also hold true for housekeeping. If housekeeping knocks on your door after 3 or 4 in the afternoon seriously think about why they would be there so late in the day. Many attackers have used maids to let them into a room. Let's face it, maid service, although a very needed profession, is not the best paid or skilled industry in some areas of the world. When housekeeping knocks on your door, walk over, look through the peep hole and make sure it actually is housekeeping along with checking to make sure that the maid is the only person standing there wanting access to the inside of your room.

Following this same reasoning, "NEVER" open the door when someone knocks on the door and says they are the *hotel manager* or *security*! There is no reason for either of these people to need access to you or your room and this is a rouse that has been used for decades to get hotel guests to unlock and open that door. If someone claims that they are the hotel manager or hotel security, ask what they want, then walk over to the desk and call the front desk to ask why this person is at your door. If it's not the hotel manager or security report it immediately; however, if for some reason you truly believe the person outside your door actually is who they claim they are and has a valid reason for speaking with you, tell them that you've just gotten out of the shower and need to get dressed. Let them know that you'll need a few minutes and that you'll meet them in the hotel lobby. After they've gone (give them several minutes), carefully look outside the door and down the hall to make sure they've actually departed and then go down stairs to meet them.

One more item on entering your hotel room: don't open or even unlock your door when someone is following you down the hall. Criminals have been known to walk down numerous hallways until they are able to slip in unnoticed behind an un-suspecting victim at the perfect time. The criminals try to time their walk to arrive just as the victim uses their room key to unlock and slightly open the door. It's at this point that the victim is shoved into the room where the door is locked behind them with the assailant inside. If someone is following you down the hall, or even coming the other direction as you approach your room, delay unlocking and opening your door until they have passed by far enough that you can enter safely and secure the door before they could arrive. It is highly unlikely that you'll be attacked standing in the hallway where other people can step outside and observe the attack as you kick, fight and scream as loud as you can to draw their attention!

Although, after reading this chapter, hotels don't seem to be safe havens for rest and relaxation, they are. If you can employ these recommended security procedures it will greatly reduce the chances of anything bad ever happening. Many of these same practices apply to living at home as they do when staying in a hotel. Don't just open your front door when the doorbell rings. Make sure you know who it is and if you don't know the person, don't open the door!

Enjoy your stay.

7

Transportation Safety

Traveling around the local area is where you start to see and enjoy the culture of the region you are visiting. In this next chapter I will discuss a number of different safety and security concerns regarding times when you'll be traveling around by ground. Whether it's on foot, taxi, bus, train, subway or private motor coach, there are a number of safety and security concerns that should be considered. Many of the recommendations in this chapter will seem like simple common sense; however, we often need a good reminder about common sense issues. In this chapter I'll not only refresh your memory about these issues, I will also provide you with a number of excellent common sense practices that I'm guessing you've never thought about before, that is until now.

Regardless of where you travel, eventually everyone will head out into the town or countryside, go out to eat in a restaurant, take in a movie or, for whatever reason, find themselves located inside a crowded building of some sort. Should some unforeseen crisis situation occur during your time in one of these establishments, like a fire, a riot or an explosion outside, statistics show that just about as many people, and in many cases more people die trying to get out of the building than they do from the actual cause of the emergency. Should you find yourself in one of these situations, I recommend two courses of action:

a) Be the first person out the door!
b) If you can't be the first person out the door, take a moment, find an alternate exit and head in that direction.

In panic situations, humans will instinctively run to the door they entered even though there may be a dozen other exits from the building. It's much like an incident inside an airplane where everyone runs for the front door where they entered. What usually happens during the panic is that everyone races for the door. The first few people get out and then someone trips, falls, gets trampled to death and then the bodies start stacking up on top of them eventually blocking the exit.

The internet video from inside the 2003 Station Night Club fire in Rhode Island demonstrates an excellent example of this. The band is playing and the crowd is rocking out to the music when the performers set off a series of pyrotechnics which set the curtains above the stage on fire. At first the audience thinks this is just part of the show. It takes nearly a minute before most people realize the danger they are in and then the situation turns into a panic. There is, in the eyes of the audience, only one way out of the building, the narrow passageway to the front door where they came in so everyone makes a rush to get there. During that panic 100 people lost their lives trying to get out that front door.[20]

If you ever find yourself inside a crowded building and for whatever reason a panic situation occurs, you want to either be one of the first people out that front door or you need to stop for just a moment and look for an alternate exit. Look around for the EXIT signs! They are posted above every exit even if the exit door is not apparent. If you are in a location that has food service, head for the kitchen. Even though it may not have an EXIT marking on the public side of the venue, all kitchens will have a back exit out of the building for taking in the food supplies they need.

---

[20] Internet video and report by the National Fire Prevention Agency, www.nfpa.org

Sometimes, if you are caught in a really large crowd that panics and moves, you'll find yourself caught in what's referred to as a flowing crowd. Just about anyone who has ever been to a major sporting event when the game is over has found themselves in this situation. The crowd is so packed together, shoulder to shoulder, that there is no way to get out of it and they must move with the flow.

If a panic situation were to occur while in this situation and you get caught in a flowing crowd, the first step to your survival is to realize that you are in a VERY dangerous situation and need to find a way out of that crowd. The way to handle it is very much like you would with a rip tide at the beach. Initially you won't have a choice but to go with the flow of the crowd and hopefully stay on your feet; however, as you move forward, try to work your way to the outside edge of the crowd. You'll find that once you've made it all the way to the outside edge you may be able to hold your position between the crowd and the wall especially when you encounter a turn or intersection. At this point you should attempt to locate an alternate way outside the facility because that crowd will eventually bunch up at the exit. Exits are always smaller and more restrictive than the hallways leading to them to facilitate entry security, not exit clearance. When this flowing crowd reaches the exit it has no choice but to congest even worse than it was previously, and, during a panic to escape, someone will fall, starting a chain reaction.

Outside the US many people travel between major cities by train. Depending on what country you are in, trains can be a fairly safe and enjoyable mode of transportation; however, in some countries trains can be anything but safe. When traveling on a train make sure to lock the door to your compartment (if you have one) and it's best to take

111

turns sleeping when traveling in a group, leaving at least one person awake to keep watch over the others.

Robberies on cross country public buses can almost be expected in some parts of the world. I've seen this happen in parts of South America on more than one occasion. The scenario goes like this: there will be 3 or 4 young thugs leaning against the back of their car sitting on the side of the road waiting for the bus to arrive. The bus driver knows the routine and he fully intends to go home at the end of the day so he grudgingly pulls over, stops and opens the door. Meanwhile the young thugs enter the bus and walk down the aisle extracting their payment for passage through their territory from each of the passengers.

Unfortunately, Americans traveling through a foreign country are basically viewed as a walking dollar sign. Many Americans traveling in foreign countries have been removed from these public buses, robbed, beaten or worse. If you decide to travel between cities on a public bus, dress down as much as possible and try as hard as you can to blend in. If you encounter a situation as described above, give the criminals anything and everything they want. There's nothing we possess that can't be replaced. This goes back to a point I made earlier about not taking anything with you that you can't afford to lose!

Choosing to rent a car to transit between locations is a very good option from a security perspective, but make sure that you select a vehicle that blends in with the other traffic in the local area. Don't choose the flashy new SUV so that you can put everyone in your party inside a single vehicle when SUVs are not as common as they are here in the US.

If SUVs or vans are not common in the country you are in, it's better to break up a large group and rent two smaller vehicles that blend in with what everyone else is driving than to stand out on the road. Many travelers have been selected as targets because they were driving the only shiny new SUV on the road.

One tactic I observed in Venezuela was very similar to the bus scenario I just talked about. Six of us were driving down a well-traveled highway in a nice new SUV when we noticed 3 young men leaning against the back of their car parked on the side of the road. Just before we passed, the young man nearest the road extended his right arm and threw a handful of tacks onto the road which we immediately ran over. Looking back we observed the men casually step into their car and begin to follow us, knowing that we would most likely experience a flat tire from a tack puncture within minutes, forcing us to pull over in a fairly remote area where we would be robbed.

Yes, this scenario really did happen with one caveat. We had a tire go down, we pulled over to the side of the road and, as expected, the car with the young thugs pulled in behind us. The caveat is that our SUV was carrying several armed federal agents from the US along with the Venezuela National Police so the ending for these three young men did not go quite as they had planned.

Renting and traveling in multiple vehicles also provides an added layer of safety. Should this scenario happen and both cars suddenly pull over, the average highway robbers would be greatly outnumbered and would probably withdraw. Additionally, if one vehicle ever breaks down in route to your destination you'll have your rescue vehicle ready and waiting.

Make sure that any vehicle you rent is in good working order, preferably with air conditioning, a locking gas tank and a good spare tire with a jack and tools. Don't skimp on a few dollars by renting vehicles from some local used car dealer. Whenever available use National Rental Car chains if at all possible.

Taxis are by far the most common form of transportation when traveling overseas or even domestically in major cities. Although not as dangerous as public buses or trains, many people are cleverly robbed by the driver while using taxis. By incorporating a few simple practices you can avoid most of these issues.

To start off, never get into a cab that is not CLEARLY marked with the company logo. I've heard countless stories from overseas mission trips, business trips and vacation travelers where they cleared customs late at the airport or walked outside a restaurant or mall to find what looked like a taxi with a driver standing outside asking if they needed a ride. Without truly considering what they were looking at, a yellow sedan that looks like a cab, they climbed inside and were subsequently driven off to a very remote location in route to their destination. The vehicle pulled into a side road or alley and suddenly stopped where the doors were opened by waiting accomplices and, if lucky, they were simply robbed and left in a very bad part of town!

Another tactic used during taxi robberies is where the driver sees you standing with your luggage, pulls up to the curb where he asks if you need a ride to the airport. The driver then lets you know that he already has a person in the back going to that same location and encourages you to hop in and split the fare. Of course the person in the back is his accomplice and you end up getting robbed or worse, never making it to your destination. Never get into a cab that already has another customer in the back! You can afford to pay for a ride to your destination on your own so, if there is someone else in the back, wait for the next vacant cab.

As I get into a taxi, I always open the door to check and make sure the door will actually open. This is another spin on the unmarked taxi scheme. The driver gets you locked in the back with the child lock system activated where you can't open the doors from the inside and then in route to the destination suddenly pulls into a secluded alley. As soon as you get inside the cab, check to see that the doors open from the inside and if not, make enough of a fuss before you leave that the driver either unlocks the doors or lets you out to catch another cab. Although it may not always work, it's better than nothing. From another perspective, you also want to make sure the doors open so that you can get out in the event you are involved in an accident.

DO NOT place your valuables in the trunk of a cab. First, you shouldn't be carrying valuables anyway, but items such as cash, passports and travel documents are valuable! Keep those items in a carry-on bag, backpack or in a pouch around your waist or neck inside the cab. When you arrive at your destination, pay the fare inside the cab and not out on the curb. You don't want to be flashing your cash around in front of the world, showing everyone how much money you have and every pick pocket exactly where you're keeping it.

Lastly, if you've placed your luggage in the trunk, do not step outside the taxi until the driver has gotten out of his seat and opened the trunk. Sounds strange? Consider this scenario; you pay inside the cab so the driver has his money, you step out onto the curb expecting the driver to follow and open the trunk only to have him drive off with all of your belongings secured in the back of his vehicle. What are you going to tell the police? NYC police report: "It was an Arab-looking man, wearing a turban around his head, driving a yellow cab." I'm sure with that information the police will figure out who that taxi driver was and get your belongings back to you in no time! Yeah right! This form of luggage theft happens every day around the world; however, if the driver has to get out and open the trunk before you get out, he can't drive off with your belongings. It's a simple practice with great results!

In big cities most people will utilize the subway or rail system to get around town. The perils of the subway have been well documented in the news and countless movies over the years and for good reason. In addition to all the good people utilizing this form of mass transit to get to work, lots of not-so-good people also use the subway system to move around town. First, when traveling on a subway try to stay in groups of 3 or more. The numbers may outweigh the risks to a would-be attacker. Second, as you start to get off at your stop take a look around and if you don't see anyone else standing around at your stop, don't get off. There is probably a darn good reason the locals have left the area! They've lived there long enough to know what danger looks like. Continue on to the next stop that has a crowd of people, get off, go upstairs and pay a taxi driver a $5 fare to take you back to your destination. You can afford the cost and inconvenience but you can't afford the alternative.

During your travels, especially on mission trips, you might be required to visit locations that may be fairly safe areas to travel through or work in during daylight hours but, can change completely as soon as the sun goes down. In every culture the criminal element is always more active after dark. Plan ahead before going into these areas and curtail your travels to daylight hours if at all possible. If you have to travel at night, anywhere at night, it's always better to stay in larger groups, on the main streets, with lots of light and lots of witnesses.

Pilots learn the importance of Situational Awareness
starting with their first day of flight training.

8

Situational Awareness

No matter where or how you travel you should always pay attention to see who might be watching you! During my travels I spend a great deal of time watching people. I find people fascinating to watch; however, in the process of watching other people I'm also trying to determine if any of them pose a threat to my safety and security.

One of the most common indicators I look for when trying to identify criminals is that they will always spend a period of time observing other people while trying to choose their next victim. Depending on the type of crime to be committed, this observation period may be only a few seconds or, as in the case of a kidnapping, may actually take place over several days. This is where paying close attention to your surroundings may give you the opportunity to detect the criminal before he strikes and to do something about it. This is the best way to prevent becoming the target of his next crime! Instead of simply avoiding the dangers, now you are actively taking a proactive approach in your own personal safety and security.

People tell me all the time, "I don't have time to sit through your entire seminar so just tell me the most important thing I need to know when traveling to: _____."

My answer: SITUATIONAL AWARENESS!

Situational Awareness: *"Being aware of and understanding everything that is happening around you."*

If you can master this one technique you will improve your own personal safety and security tenfold. But it's not always as easy as it might sound, especially when you get outside your comfort zone like traveling on that subway, walking down the street in a crowd, working in a very poor run-down section of town or maybe in some refugee camp. When people get outside their comfort zone, their natural tendency is to get tunnel vision. This is the brain's own defense mechanism and a subconscious way of coping with very uncomfortable surroundings. When people feel threatened or find themselves in a situation that is very foreign, as compared to their routine life back home, they tend to focus and concentrate on whatever is directly in front of them and instinctively tune out everything else. This way their mind doesn't have to think about what might be going on around them. Unfortunately, this is just the opposite of what you should be doing.

If you ever find yourself in a situation where you suddenly experience what we call "tunnel vision" where, in a protective mode, your mind has begun to filter out everything happening in your periphery, stop for a moment. Look around and observe what is going on around you. Your brain may have received some sort of intuition alert of impending danger which caused this to happen. Maybe there is something wrong that you need to be aware of or maybe it's nothing more than the crowds pushing in around you in an unfamiliar place. Regardless, it's better to be safe than sorry so take a minute and look around. You might suddenly realize that someone is staring directly at you and watching everything you're doing and I don't mean in just a curious manner.

But let's say this happens when you are seriously involved in some task where you cannot take your attention away from the issue at hand to see why you are suddenly getting tunnel vision. If you are traveling with a companion, ask him or her to look around and make sure everything is okay. If that intuitive alert continues to make you feel uneasy and you cannot find the source of your intuitive feeling, then it's time to move and get out of that area. What's the worst that can happen? You'll lose a few minutes of time leaving and then coming back when you know it's safe.

Use the subway scenario as an example. Most people who are robbed as they are leaving the subway have been watched for quite some time. The victims were chosen, observed and then followed. Regardless of where you are or what you are doing, if you notice someone paying far too much attention to you, move and be observant. Did they follow when you moved? If so, move again and if they follow you a second time, go directly to a place of safety!

Another option before you even get to this point is to basically call them out visually. If you observe someone watching you, look directly back at them. People who are simply noticing someone from a foreign country will slowly look away, it's a natural tendency when eye contact is made; however, anyone who has a more sinister reason for watching you will feel that they have been caught and will abruptly turn away. It's this *quick* break in eye contact that usually gives away someone with criminal intent. As this person looks back, and he will, let him know that he's been caught. Visually scan and observe him from head to toe as if making a mental note of everything: what they are wearing, scars, hats or jewelry. Criminals don't want you to be able to identify them to the police, so if you give them this stare down it's as though you're letting them know that you are not going to be a passive victim and hopefully they will move on to someone else.

One of my biggest goals in writing this book is to get people to look at the world a little more like a police officer does. As I discussed in the very first chapter, this all comes down to perception. If you are made aware of the dangers that are truly out there, and if the time comes where you are presented with that real life experience of coming into contact with an actual threat, hopefully you'll be able to utilize the knowledge you've learned in this book and be able to take action, avoid the dangers involved in that situation and not be part of next year's statistics.

Let's use the simple example of you and a police officer both stopping at a convenience store to buy a cup of coffee. You'll pull into the parking lot, walk into the store, retrieve a cup, fill it with coffee, walk over and pay the clerk and then return to your car.

Because of a police officer's training and experience, his perception of convenience stores is a little different from yours. He knows that less than desirable people sometimes hang out in these establishments for several minutes before they rob the store. Who hasn't heard about the local convenience store getting robbed?

So the police officer pulls in to get a cup of coffee, parks his car, walks into the store and then he will take just a moment to look up and down the aisles to see who's there. If there are no other customers or at least none that seem threatening, he will walk over, pour that same cup of coffee, pay the clerk and then leave. However, if, when he walks into the store and looks around, he notices a couple of young people who look like they are from one of the local gangs walking around or standing in the aisles not seeming very interested in making a quick selection from the shelves, that police officer will most likely either stand there and observe their actions for a while (because it's his job) or he will walk outside and sit in his car until these suspicious customers leave.

This is the same type of situational awareness that I hope to pass on to you, not just during your trip to the convenience store but throughout life. If you understand what to look for and don't see it, you won't have any fear and will continue on with your planned activities. On the other hand, if you walk in and danger is present, by being taught what to look for, the innate functions of your brain should sound the alarm. You'll notice the danger, turn around and get out of the store!

Again, I like the example Gavin De Becker used in his book *The Gift of Fear* for this very scenario to explain how intuition works. Robert Thompson was an airline pilot in Atlanta when he stopped at a convenience store on his way to work. The following day Mr. Thompson was called in to talk to police about what happened at the store and he made the following statements: "I walked into the convenience store to buy a few magazines and for some reason I was suddenly.....afraid. It was just a gut feeling so I turned right around and walked out."

The danger signals in Mr. Thompson's brain sounded and his intuition kicked in! He had no idea why but he followed his instinct and left the store. Good job!

He continues, "Well, now that I think back, the guy behind the counter looked at me with a very rapid glance, just jerked his head toward me for an instant. I guess I'm used to the clerk sizing you up when you walk in, but he was intently looking at another customer. He was focused on a customer who was wearing a big heavy jacket and of course now I realize that it was very hot."

Intuition is amazing! Your brain can process input at a rate that is off the scale as compared to your mind being able to comprehend all of the information your senses take in. When you get that sudden feeling that something is not right, please don't hesitate to figure out what it is, just turn around and walk out the door. Move! What if you're wrong and there was nothing there? Okay, you had to drive two blocks down the road to the next convenience store and lost two minutes of your time. Then again, if your intuition was right, that two minutes may have save your life.

Unfortunately, the police officer who walked into that convenience store just moments after Robert Thompson walked out missed those same intuitive signals from the clerk. Unfortunately, he did not notice the two gang members standing in the back of the store wearing long coats on that warm evening. They were there to rob the store and he was fatally shot before he detected the threat.

This book is about international travel for mission trips but honestly, most of the safety and security tips I've included to this point would apply to taking your spouse out to dinner in the average city here in America just as much as it does traveling into some foreign land. These are simply good practices to incorporate into your daily lives no matter where you live or where you travel.

Let's take the issue of sexual assault as just one example of the dangers we face every day right here at home. On average, in America during every hour, 75 women will be raped which means that during my average seminar on international travel safety and security the lives of approximately 300 women will be tragically changed forever.

Fortunately statistics like these can be greatly reduced by taking a proactive approach to your personal security and always maintaining good situational awareness. You'll actually find that the world is much more interesting once you start to take it all in and you will be far less fearful than when you walked through life blindly. When you walk through life being aware of what is happening around you, you're not afraid.

Regardless of where you go or what you do, always pay attention when you see someone looking at you. Unless the person is a *trained* professional, you'll be able to determine very quickly whether or not something is wrong. If it seems inappropriate, move. If he follows you, then move again and if he follows you a second time, go as fast as you can to the nearest safety zone with lots of witnesses.

My brother is a wonderful man and a professional musician who has played and toured internationally with groups like the Atlanta Pops and the rock group "Truth" for many years. He loves to visit big cities and travels all over the world. Unfortunately, his situational awareness has been down a few times and he's been mugged and badly injured on more than one occasion.

During one of my business trips I stopped in to see my brother and was explaining to him this concept of situational awareness and paying attention to who is watching and especially following you. We decided to take a break and walk downtown to get a late breakfast. As we (2 males) rounded the corner onto a larger street, we stepped in line behind a young lady who was obviously out for a morning exercise walk. We ended up approximately 20 feet behind this woman traveling in the same direction and she almost immediately walked across to the sidewalk on the other side of the street.

I explained to my brother that this was the exact behavior that I needed him to learn and follow. Of course he knew we were no threat to this lady and he couldn't believe that the woman's actions were taken on our account, so at my suggestion we crossed the street. This was followed by the woman looking over her shoulder at us and immediately crossing back to the side where we had all just come from. My brother was amazed that someone would actually do that, but I wasn't. She was obviously a well-educated, security-minded person who paid attention to what was happening around her. Then my brother suggested that we cross the street again to see what she would do, at which time I explained that she was out for an exercise walk and I had no intention of changing that to what she would certainly perceive as a sprint for her life!

The point was made. Pay attention to what is going on around you and if you believe someone may be following you, do something to confirm it, and if they are, MOVE immediately to a place of safety!

This habit of observing everything that is happening around you is even more important when working in a foreign country. Foreigners are often looked at by the criminal element as a walking dollar sign.

Let's consider for a moment the perspective of Americans from the criminal's point of view:

1. Americans have money! And it is true, even if you are the poorest college student out on a spring break vacation you probably have more money with you than most people in that country make in a month or even a year and if you don't have money, your family certainly does.

2. You probably don't speak the local language well enough to fully communicate what has happened and probably have no idea how to contact the police.

3. Even if you are able to contact the police, file the report and this person gets arrested for his crime, it is very unlikely that you will be there to testify in court when his trial comes up and therefore he will be set free.

4. Lastly, if this criminal is not looking for a quick robbery but rather has more grandiose ideas, you, the American, are worth a very nice ransom to your church, organization or your family. Kidnapping in some countries is a full-time enterprise with vast financial rewards and very little risk.

If you will honestly consider what Americans are from the criminal's point of view, you'll understand why we need to keep our situational awareness at its highest level at all times. We are EASY targets who are walking around their country often making trouble for their way of life.

So what should we be looking for? Basically anything that looks wrong or out of place. If it looks wrong it probably is! Have you ever had the hair on the back of your neck stand on end for no apparent reason? Sure, we all have. That's intuition at its highest physical level and it was based on something that your subconscious mind noticed but your brain didn't fully process.

Have you ever found yourself in a situation where you got a sudden feeling like something was wrong, turned down a side street, entered a building or found yourself anywhere when your intuition turned on to let you know that something was not right but didn't have any idea why? When you find yourself in one of these situations, do exactly as Robert Thompson did: turn around and get out of there as fast as you can. Your subconscious mind has picked up the clues and your intuition is letting you know that something is wrong. Once you've reached a safe location, then figure out what you should do next.

What about the scenario where several of you get that uneasy intuitive feeling that something is wrong as you are walking down the road into the neighborhood where your team will be working? Not going down there may not be an option. First, back out of that location to a place of safety where you can consider the security issues presented in this location. If it looks like a bad area then it is a bad area but that doesn't mean that you don't go in there. After all, going down that street to work is why you traveled half way around the world in the first place. It just means that you walk in better prepared and wiser.

Consider this option for the scenario: back out and call the manager at the facility down that road and ask him or her to come to your hotel for a talk. Be open about your security concerns. Locals know the area and they will usually know the dangers, even those you may not be aware of, and will fully understand your concerns.

If they have a good working relationship with the neighbors, it might be a good idea to ask them or one of the local employees to walk you into the neighborhood and introduce you to everyone, and I do mean everyone! Americans hardly know their neighbor's names; however, in most foreign countries, people who live in neighborhoods have probably lived there their entire lives and know everyone else who lives there, both good and bad. As this person walks you through the neighborhood, have him introduce you and tell everyone who you are and what you will be doing. "These people came from America and will be here working at our facility for the next two weeks. Please keep an eye on them for me." These locals know who the trouble makers are and by simply being introduced they are much more likely to say something when you are being watched or followed.

I said that you should be introduced to everyone and that includes the bad elements in the neighborhood as well. If this person sees some of the local trouble makers, points them out and even introduces you to them, then:

   a) you know who these people are, and

   b) they know you know who they are!

You are now able to identify the attackers should they try something and now they are aware of this fact. These criminals are less likely to choose you as a victim and more likely to look for another target who can't identify them.

During a career in federal law enforcement, especially as a pilot flying overhead where you can see the movements of the suspects and all of the police surveillance vehicles following the suspects, you can always tell who is well versed in surveillance techniques and who is new to the game. It takes several years of practicing good surveillance techniques before it becomes natural and virtually undetectable by the suspect. Until then just about everyone makes the same basic mistakes. These common surveillance mistakes become very obvious once you know what to look for and it is quite easy to determine if some untrained person is following you.

I'll cover the most common mistakes made during surveillances, not because I think you'll be followed by the police, but because criminals make these same mistakes. If you are being followed by the criminal element in a country as they are choosing their next victim, you'll be able to detect it, change directions and get some place safe where you can make good security choices on what you should do next.

1. Pay attention to any vehicle that pulls out into traffic at the same time you do. This would apply to leaving a location by foot as well. Does anyone start walking or driving in the same direction at the same time you do and do they suddenly stop when you stop?

2. Do they drive or walk too fast trying to catch up when they get behind or suddenly slow down when you do or make an abrupt stop for no apparent reason? Are their movements erratic? People trying to follow someone are often quite

obvious by their movements because they don't know what that person is going to do next.

3. Do these people, who started out at the same time you did, stay the same distance from you all the time? If you speed up, do they speed up? If you suddenly slow down, do they suddenly slow down, all the while maintaining approximately the same distance in trail (their comfort distance from the target)?

4. Are they constantly looking at you? This may sound a little funny because lots of people look at you but not like they do when someone is intentionally surveilling someone. This is the most obvious thing you'll notice if someone is intentionally following you. As a vehicle pulls up beside you, both heads are turned and looking directly at you and as you pull away, their eyes (faces) seem to be tracking your every move. It's hard to follow someone without actually watching them.

One common tactic used in many foreign countries for payoffs, robberies and even kidnappings is what I like to call the Bump-N-Rob or the Bump-N-Grab. I've seen this scenario happen several times over the years in a number of different countries. The criminals will follow the foreigners waiting for just the right location, with few or no witnesses, at which time they will simply pull up and bump the back bumper of your vehicle expecting you to simply pull over. They will often play up the acting part by appearing to be sorry and waiving you to the side of the road where, of course, things don't quite go as you thought they would. After you pull over in this remote location, these criminals either rob or kidnap their victims.

Should this vehicle bump ever happen to you, remember your situational awareness training before you consider what actions to take. Where are you? Who is in the other car, an older couple or three young men? Are you in a safe location with good lighting and lots of witnesses? If the passengers in the other vehicle look harmless "and" you are in a safe, well-lit location with lots of witnesses, pull over and see if this was an innocent accident; however, if you are not in a good location or the occupants of the other vehicle don't look so harmless, DO NOT pull over, at least not right there. Even if the other driver starts blowing his horn and making a fuss, maybe especially in this situation, continue driving until you reach a location where you feel comfortable, some place safe with lights and witnesses, and then pull over. One of the best locations would be directly in front of the local police station! You can always explain your case and security concerns to the police officer. A crowded mall, a hospital or local church would be other good options.

Do you know where these safe locations are located in the areas you'll be working or visiting? In the next chapter on foreign travel planning we'll discuss this issue in a little more detail. One thing I tell everyone before going overseas is to conduct a little research on the local area where you will be working and staying. Know the location of the nearest police station, the hospital, mall, etc. in relationship to where you'll be staying and working. These safe locations should be identified even before you arrive.

Back to being followed: if you even think that you are being followed, do something to confirm it much like the woman did crossing the street when my brother and I stepped out behind her. I like to say that 3 rights make a wrong (you can go right or left). Whether walking or driving, if you think even for a second that you are being followed, turn right at the next intersection. If that person makes the same right turn, make another right. Now you've made a U-turn and are heading back in the direction you came from. Of course, just maybe they needed to head back the same direction as well, so if they are still back there make a third right turn. Now you've gone around the block and are going back to the same street you started on.

There is NO reason for someone to circle the block in the exact same direction you did at the exact same time. If this happens trust me, YOU ARE being followed!
So what should you do next? Don't stop, don't speed up or give any indication that you realize something is wrong until you reach your safe house, preferably a police station. This simple act may very well save your life.

Okay, let's say you have been followed by someone. Now what should you do? It's time to get somewhere safe and make a serious change in your security plans! At a minimum you and your party need to consider changing hotels. Also change the routes you travel to and from the place you are staying as well as to the locations where you are working. You should consider changing what you are doing and where you are going. This should include the possibility of heading home.

These and many other possibilities need to be discussed openly with everyone in your party, and you should be prepared for the different viewpoints regarding your situation. Some people will deny that anything has happened or that there is any danger to the safety of your party. Some will override the evidence and want to move forward with their planned activities with little, if any, changes while others will want to pack up and head home right then and there.

What is the right decision? It all depends on where you are, what happened and how that information correlates to the security threats you found for that country during your research on the area before you left home. In the next chapter I will cover where and how to do the pre-travel research.

First and foremost, you must openly admit one fact: You have been targeted for a reason and you don't want to end up being a victim! Take that proactive approach to your personal security and don't just sit back and let something bad happen to you and your traveling companions. "Remember," you're responsible for your own safety!

Here is a good example: George was a successful businessman working on a temporary contract for his company in east Africa. He stayed in a very nice, fully furnished apartment the company had set up for him. He had a driver pick him up at exactly 8:15 every morning and take him to the job site.

One day as they were traveling along the same route they took every day, a white sedan with three men inside pulled out from a side street as they approached and blocked the road. George's driver slammed on his brakes and slid to a stop just inches from the other car, cursing and yelling at the other driver to get out of the way. Before the driver realized what was happening, three men got out of the sedan with guns drawn and took George hostage.

After two months in captivity, George's company paid the one million dollar ransom (in local currency, about $22,000 US) and secured his release. During his debrief with authorities George made an interesting statement. About three to four weeks after his abduction, George realized that the day before he was actually taken hostage, the exact same group of abductors attempted to kidnap him in the exact same location, at exactly the same time of day. George and his driver had set a very predictable pattern which made the kidnapping very easy for his abductors. George and his driver had ignored the warning signs.

One day while sitting in his holding room with nothing to do but think, George suddenly remembered that the day before his kidnapping, as his driver was heading down that same road, that same white sedan loaded with those same three men suddenly pulled out into the street in front of them. George's driver nearly plowed right into the other vehicle. Fortunately, George's driver was able to quickly swerve to the side avoiding the collision and as they passed the kidnappers George's driver shouted and called them just about every name in the book! They both thought that the operator of the other car was nothing more than a bad driver who almost caused an accident. They didn't realize or didn't want to realize what had almost taken place.

Now that George had nothing more to do than think, he remembered the car pulling out and intentionally blocking the road the day before, those same three men in the car and the two men opening their doors to get out holding what he now realized were AK47s. George's driver went around the obstacle so quickly that neither of them took the time to pay attention to what was really happening. At the time of the incident it just didn't click in George's mind as being a security threat. The possibility of being kidnapped

135

was something he had never seriously considered, so George and his driver followed their same daily routine making it easy to be taken hostage in that same location, by the same men, driving the same white sedan, at the same time the following day. Had George been practicing good situational awareness and taken in the whole picture of what happened they could have made changes to their routine, left earlier for work the next day, taken a different route to the job site and avoided becoming a victim.

So, hypothetically, what would you do if you found yourself in the same situation as George, the difference being that you were behind the steering wheel and not some paid driver? First of all, I recommend that you always leave at least one car length of space between you and the vehicle you are following. This space will allow you to turn and maneuver around most hazards. Of course, in many locations, let's take Sao Paulo, Brazil as an example, leaving a car length of space between you and the vehicle in front of you is like opening a free passing lane where countless vehicles will fill the void and you'll never get anywhere, but whenever possible don't just pull up on the bumper of the car in front of you. Leave some room for safety. I even do this in the drive-through lane at fast food restaurants which of course makes everyone behind me mad, but I like to know that if I need to get out of that line during an emergency I can.

Let's go back and place you in George's situation. You're driving down the road and another vehicle pulls out and blocks the road. It's one of the most common kidnapping maneuvers in the world and I've met several people who have witnessed this event. So what do you do? First and foremost you have to maintain your situational awareness and quickly determine what is going on. Is this a possible kidnapping or was it simply a bad driver? Take a moment to look around at what is happening beside and behind you? If in fact this is an abduction in progress, your best bet is to attempt to get away by either backing up (if another vehicle hasn't blocked you from the rear, which is a common tactic,) driving around the blocker as George's driver did the day before, or you might consider moving that blocking vehicle out of the way.

If there is enough room to maneuver around the blocking vehicle you can drive over the curb, over any shrubbery, and make your own way out of the situation to some place safe. This is not the time to obey all the traffic rules; you are in a survival situation.

There are a few rules you need to know about jumping over a curb in a passenger car. First, you need to be going slower than 35 mph. Speeds over 35-40 mph will probably do enough damage to the suspension of the vehicle that you may not be able to drive away. Second, you'll need to drive over the curb at a 30 to 45 degree angle. Much less of an angle than this and many cars will simply bounce off the curb and back into the street. Angles in excess of 45 degrees will often bounce the car so violently that it does major damage to the undercarriage of the vehicle. Of course, if you have no other choice but to hit the curb going too fast or at a different angle, you take what you can get. This is a survival situation and anything goes. If you make it, great; if not, there is certainly no harm in trying. Even if you do it perfectly you'll need to get a new front end alignment regardless of speed, but that's a small price to pay.

Another option, especially if there is no room or no way to drive around the blocking vehicle, is to simply move the other vehicle out of the way. It's really not that hard "IF" you know what to do.

Just about every police officer learns the PIT (pursuit intervention technique) maneuver early on in his or her career and you've probably seen it done on TV countless times during news releases of police car chases. There are a few bits and pieces of information you need to know in order to do it correctly. To start with, you never want to ram the middle of the other vehicle. This will only push the other car down the street and not move it out of the way. What you want to do is aim the corner of your car at either the front or rear axle of the other vehicle. Aim at their wheels with the corner of your vehicle and drive into the other car. The blocking vehicle will spin out of your way with very little effort. As it starts to move out of the way you want to continue *driving straight ahead.* As soon as you clear the obstacle, head immediately to the nearest safe location and get help. *Now it is time to pack quickly and go home!*

In following chapters I am going to talk specifically about foreign travel. Up to this point just about everything I've discussed could apply to your everyday life as well as it would for traveling to some exotic foreign location. It's a lot to take in and many people around this point will start to think that either life is full of nothing but dangers or that I am trying to scare people, which is certainly not the case. Let's put all of this information into its proper perspective.

When was the last time you took a vacation to some tropical beach? A good percentage of you have gone to the beach and laid out enjoying the sun with the waves breaking over the sand and the tropical breeze flowing through your hair. There is, however, a hidden danger on most tropical beaches that people never stop to consider. It kills more people each year than shark attacks, rip tides and Portuguese manta war jelly fish all combined. Thousands of people have been killed, seriously injured, maimed and disfigured for life by injuries from this serious threat to your safety. What is it, you ask? The coconut! Yes, you read it right, the common every day coconut.

On average, every year around the world 150 people are killed by coconuts falling out of palm trees and thousands more are very seriously injured by these deadly weapons.[21] Think about what they actually are from a danger perspective for just a minute. Remember the last time you walked out on that sandy beach and you saw lying on the ground dozens of coconuts? These 4 to 6-pound rock-hard objects grow at heights of around 80 feet and falling from that height causes them to reach speeds of around 50 mph. Can you imagine getting hit by a 6-pound rock traveling at 50 miles per hour? What kind of damage do you think that would do to your body? Every one of those coconuts lying on the beach fell out of that tree within the past few weeks and if anyone had decided to place their beach towel or lawn chair in the shade of the nearest coconut palm tree when the coconut fell -- well, you get the idea.

So how do you combat this serious danger? It's so simple! (A guy named Newton actually figured this one out!) When you walk out on the beach and are looking for a place to spread out your beach towel, take a quick look around and see if there are any coconuts lying nearby. If so, look up and see if there are any left up in the tree. It's a simple matter of gravity and direction. The coconuts in the tree will eventually fall down, straight down, so simply

---

[21] https://en.wikipedia.org/wiki/Death_by_coconut

move your towel over a few feet so that you are not directly underneath the tree. It's that simple.

What about all the information I've been presenting to you in the book up to this point? It's simple, it's mostly common sense and it's no different than paying attention to the coconuts. Employ a few simple safety and security related practices into your daily lives and you can eliminate getting hit by the majority of the "coconuts." Once you know the information and you know what to look for, your eyes will be opened to the dangers and your brain will automatically tell you that you're standing underneath the "coconut tree."

Proverbs 27-12 NLT

"A prudent person foresees danger and takes precautions. The simpleton goes blindly on and suffers the consequences."

I like the way Andy Stanley, pastor of Northpoint Church in Atlanta incorporates this philosophy. Referencing Solomon's wisdom in Proverbs 27-12 he states:

"Drawing on their own experiences or the experience of others, the prudent anticipate the future and choose accordingly." "They draw upon the wealth of data that life has already provided and then take appropriate action when they see danger ahead."

Andy follows this with a great prayer on Situational Awareness: *"Lord, help us to see trouble coming long before it gets here and give us the wisdom to know what to do and the courage to do it."*

9

Active Shooter

In recent years the media has changed the type of stories it likes to present. BREAKING NEWS is what grabs the audience's attention and few stories will do that quicker than an active shooter. With this model of storyline, it seems like active shooting situations have significantly increased over the past decade. Events such as Sandy Hook Elementary, the college shooting in Umpqua Oregon, the movie theater in Denver as well as the office Christmas party attack by Islamic terrorists in San Bernardino, CA *seem* to happen almost every week. In reality, active shooter situations are not a new phenomenon. Many of you may remember the derogatory term "Going Postal." Twenty five years ago there were a number of well publicized active shooter events involving mass casualties committed by postal workers at U.S. postal facilities. Unfortunately, this was the beginning of the use of sensationalized media, which in turn spurred many copycat incidents as well as giving credence to the depraved minds of the individuals which they believed gave them national recognition for their heinous acts.

The United States is a very modern country and was formed after the invention of the modern firearm, hence forth America developed as a gun culture. Even our founding fathers included our right to bear arms in the second amendment of our constitution. Most countries around the world developed thousands of years earlier and are more of a knife culture (knives, swords, machete's, etc.) where you are more likely to be robbed by someone threatening you with a blade than you are a gun. Conversely, here in America, you are more likely to be confronted by someone holding a gun than you are a knife.

This does not mean that you won't have your life threatened by someone holding a gun in some foreign country, especially during some sort of terrorist incident, but most common criminals in other countries continue to favor the blade. This is also due in some degree to the criminal penalties associated with firearms vs. knives and the availability of firearms.

Take our neighbor to the north for instance. In Canada it is a felony to be in possession of a handgun. With the exception of law enforcement, the only hand guns in Canada were smuggled into the country. Conversely, in America you can just walk into any sporting goods store or pawn shop and purchase a pistol in an hour or two with a minimum of paperwork and proper identification.

Houses of worship here in the U.S. are certainly not immune to the active shooter event. Some of the more publicized church shootings, such as the 2015 prayer meeting in Charleston SC, the 2007 shootings at New Life Church Colorado Springs and the YWAM camp in Denver are a stark reminder that no place is immune to active shooter situations.

Carl Chinn tracks and provides one of the best sources on church violence statistics.[22] Over the past 15 years there have been over 1000 shootings in U.S. churches with more than 550 fatalities. Mr. Chinn's records show that 2014, being the last year updated, has been the worst year on record with 176 shootings and 74 fatalities in U.S. churches. The U.S. Department of Labor reports a yearly average of over 550 shootings happen in workplaces around our country every year.[23]

---

[22] www.carlchinn.com
[23] http://www.bls.gov/iif/oshwc/cfoi/osar0016.htm

144

I bring these statistics up to make you aware that the media only publicizes a very small portion of the active shooter incidents our country faces virtually every day. The point of this chapter is to inform you, the reader, of the dangers and knowledgeable on proper procedures should you encounter an active shooter situation.

It doesn't matter if you are at work, church, school, a hotel or even visiting a mall in Africa on the last day of your mission trip (remember the West Gate Mall incident in Nairobi Kenya?) No matter where you are, the proper procedures to follow during an active shooter incident are all the same!

A lot of miss information has been publicized in years past regarding active shooter responses and many people, even administrators at our schools and churches are still following old, outdated and ineffective practices. They tend to follow the policy of **"Lock Down"** as the only response to an active shooter situation. This was the general thinking of law enforcement around the country until the Columbine High School shooting took place in 1999. Police tactics called for officers to surround a building with an active shooter inside and then begin negotiations to have the shooter give up and come out. That practice has proven time and time again to be inappropriate with a huge cost in lives lost.

For employees and visitors, the general thinking up to that point was to lock down the facility with everyone inside and wait for law enforcement to arrive. The problem is, even with the new updated law enforcement tactics, the average time for the police to respond and enter the building is 5 to 10 minutes as policy requires that a minimum of three officers must be on scene before they can enter a facility with an active shooter threat. The issue is that most, in fact almost all active shooter situations are over in 3 to 5 minutes which is generally before the police arrive.

So who is responsible for protecting you and those around you should you be involved in an active shooter situation?

YOU!

That's right, you. By the time the police arrive and respond to stop the threat, the incident is usually over. So if lock down is not the correct procedure, what is?

To start with, yes, the Lock Down procedure works, but *ONLY* when the threat is *OUTSIDE* the building! If the threat from a person with a firearm is outside the building you want to keep them there and keep yourself, and any others, safe inside the building; however, the instant that threat makes it through any door and is now inside the facility, Lock Down no longer applies.

The correct response actually consists of three parts:
RUN, HIDE and FIGHT.

After the ineffective response to the shooting at Columbine high school, law enforcement agencies have done a fair job in training their officers on the new tactics to be employed in stopping an active shooter. The problem is that active shooter events are usually over before police arrived so anyone that finds themselves involved in an active shooter situation has to rely on themselves to survive the event.

In 2012 the FBI, in cooperation with the Dept. of Homeland Security, produced a training video entitled

Surviving the Active Shooter Event.[24] You can find this video posted on their agency websites and on youtube.com. It was produced because the general public was not receiving information on the proper response to these events which changed after Columbine. The video is intended to educate the general public about the proper three part procedures to follow and get everyone away from the old "lock down" mind set.

RUN, HIDE, FIGHT

RUN – Once the threat from someone with a weapon is inside the same building you are in, if you are able to get out of the building, *RUN* and get out as fast as you can.

It doesn't matter where you are or what you are doing, if you hear anything that sounds like gun shots, don't wait for everyone else to do something, leave! Also consider the fact that gun shots down the hall, around the corner or on another floor of a building can be audible but may not have that loud crack of a gun shot fired nearby. Many people who have not attended any sort of active shooter training disregard gun shots as street traffic or construction noise until it's too late. If something sounds even vaguely like gunfire leave the building if at all possible. What's the worst that will happen if you're wrong, you'll lose fifteen minutes of productivity? I'll take that over the alternative any day!

Which direction should you run? Often businesses, schools and even churches will have set evacuation procedures such as those used during a fire drill. In the event of an active shooter evacuation their policy calls for everyone to walk

---

[24] www.fbi.gov/about-us/office-of-partner-engagement/active-shooter-incidents/run-hide-fight-video

in an orderly fashion out of the building through the front entry door.

In an active shooter situation you *RUN away* from the sound of the gun fire as fast as you can! Let's face it, most shooters walk in the front door of the building. If the threat is in the front of the building, go out the back, if the threat is on one end of the building, go out the other.

The news video from the 2015 terrorist shootings at the Bataclan concert hall in Paris gives a clear demonstration of this procedure with patrons of the concert climbing out balcony doors, windows and fire escapes to flee the massacre happening inside.[25] If you are truly facing someone with a weapon shooting people inside the facility, get out as fast as you can, any way you can.

Once outside where should you go? Answer, away from the building and out of range of the firearm. Organizations today should be proactive and periodically practice active shooter drills just like we do the annual fire drill. These drills need to include the location of designated rally points located in multiple directions where everyone can meet. Rally points should be off the facility property far enough that the people escaping are safe and won't be confronted by the shooter as he or she is trying to leave the facility.

HIDE – If you are not able to get out of the building then your second option is to get out of site and *HIDE*. Often the only way to reach an exit is to step out into a hallway in front of the shooter so in that case you want to get out of site and try to keep the shooter out of the area you're hiding

---

[25] www.cnn.com/videos/world/2015/11/14/bataclan-concert-hall-hostages-flee-video.cnn/video/playlists/paris-shootings/

in. Yes, this is similar to the lock down procedures with a few added measures.

If you are in an area with lots of other people, spread out and do not stay huddled in a group. I'm not saying anything bad about the teachers at Sandy Hook Elementary but all 20 children who were shot and killed were huddled together in a small group inside the classroom.[26] The teacher was doing what she had been taught for a lock down procedure; however, when Adam Lanza stepped into that classroom, all of his targets (yes, that's the way he viewed those children) were grouped tightly together and he was quickly able to shoot and kill every one. Had those children been spread out and hidden as best they could within that room, it would have at least taken longer for him to locate his intended targets.

The next time you're sitting at your office desk, look around and think about where you could hide if you heard gun shots and there was no way to exit the building. Storage closets, behind boxes, under your desk with the chair tucked in and a coat covering your body or maybe inside a large cabinet could be good hiding places.

If you are hiding inside a room of any type, if equipped, lock the door. Active shooters are usually in quite a hurry to get in, do as much damage as possible and get out. If they come across a locked door they will often continue on to other parts of the facility. In addition to the lock or if there is no lock installed, try to block the door.

In an earlier chapter on hotel safety I talked about the Wedgeit, a door blocking device that I use to keep someone from entering my hotel room even if they have a key. I've

---

[26] www.en.wikipedia.org/wiki/Sandy_Hook_Elementary_School_shooting

had hundreds of office workers, school and Sunday school teachers acquire Wedgeits for active shooter protection. If the shooter can't get through the door to where you're hiding, you're probably not going to get shot.

While hidden, make sure you silence your cell phone. Columbine was another example where this became an issue. Students at Columbine who could not get out of the building, hid anywhere they could. Friends and family of the students began calling their cell phones to find out if they were okay. As Dylan Klebold and Eric Harris wandered the hallways of the school looking for more victims they actually heard cell phones ring which led them directly to their next victims.[27] Silence you phone.

If at all possible, call 911 and notify the police of an active shooter situation. Don't assume that someone else has already called. The sooner the police are notified, the sooner they will arrive. Just make sure the shooter is far enough away that you won't be heard. Give the 911 operator as much information as you can, where you are, where the shooter is, any description that you might have: gender, race, clothing, type of weapon, etc.

FIGHT – The third phase of an active shooter response is to *FI*GHT it out with the shooter. In the same response as I recommended for a terrorist hijacking, I'd rather go down fighting with a possible chance of stopping the threat than to simply stand there and die!

If you can't get out of the building and are hiding from the threat, prepare yourself and those around you to *FIGHT* should the shooter make it into the location where you are. In the same way I asked you to look around the next time

---

[27] Columbine by Dave Cullen

you're sitting at your desk and see where you could possibly hide, I'd also like you to look around and see what you have that could be used as a weapon. Office scissors, chairs, briefcases can all be used as make shift weapons to deter or subdue a threat.

When I talk to teachers and Sunday school volunteers I tell them that, if faced with an active shooter situation, to prepare their children to follow their lead and fight should the shooter make it through the door. Imagine the situation I described earlier at Sandy Hook Elementary with the students huddled in their classroom. They heard the gun shots and knew a shooter was inside the building. If the teacher had prepared her students to fight, told them that when the shooter stepped through the door that she would charge and hit him with a chair and that no matter what they saw or what happened, they were to rush him, hit him with their backpacks and then run outside the building, what would have happened?

Adam Lanza had to stop and reload his weapon before he could finish killing the teacher and all 20 of those children. If, after the teacher was shot and killed, those children had been able to hit him with 20 backpacks while running for the door, I don't believe we would have lost every student that was inside that classroom. Some yes, all probably not.

But what if you don't have time to Run or Hide? For many people in the earlier referenced incidents, that was exactly the situation. As with the Emanuel AME Church in Charleston, Dylann Roof had been sitting in that prayer meeting for quite a while before pulling out his pistol, shooting and killing 9 of the 12 people present.[28] In this situation there was no time to run, no opportunity to hide,

---

[28] www.en.wikipedia.org/wiki/Charleston_church_shooting

everyone there had only one option and that was to *FIGHT*, immediately!

It's extremely difficult for an unarmed person to attack someone holding a gun but if you find yourself confronted with this situation there is no other choice. I am not talking about the situation where someone with a gun is trying to relieve you of your wallet, purse or nice watch and then walk away. I'm specifically talking about an active shooter situation where they are intent on killing innocent people. In this situation it's either fight with the possibility of living (being able to run to safety) or dying where you stand. As I said before, I'd rather die fighting.

When the police show up you need to understand that they are not there, at least initially, to rescue you. The police are there to stop the shooter from killing other people. They also don't know exactly who the shooter is and who you are. Many criminals and terrorist have escaped or at least attempted to escape the scene by blending in with the victims and walking out the front door right past the police.

As the police reach your area make sure that your hands are clearly visible. The best option is to hold them above or on top of your head. This is the most non-threatening position to a police officer. If you have any details about the shooter provide them to the police: where the shooter is/was, gender, a description of their clothing, physical attributes and type of weapon.

Many active shooter incidents have turned into hostage situations as the events unfolded (I'll go into surviving a hostage situation later in this book.) How do you know the difference? If the shooter is present and he/she stops shooting, it may be turning into a situation where they want to live and hopefully get away. This usually won't happen in a terrorist type of shooting but does often happen in a workplace, school or church shooting.

Hostage takers want to achieve a goal, usually to live. It's best to remain calm, follow any directions that you are given and wait for law enforcement officials to resolve the issue; however, be prepared for the situation to turn back into a shooting scenario. If the shooter feels like he/she will die regardless of what they do or come to the realization that they will spend the rest of their lives in prison, they may snap and go back to killing as many victims as they can before either killing themselves or letting law enforcement do it for them, death by cop as it's called is a common way for cowards to commit suicide.

After any attack, do not wait for medical personnel to arrive before treating wounded victims. Law enforcement will not let medical personnel into the area until they are absolutely certain that all threats have been neutralized. In many cases the police have received conflicting reports or descriptions of the shooter from different sources and may believe that more than one shooter was involved in the incident. In these cases, medical personnel have been delayed from reaching the victims for hours. If you or personnel around you have had any medical training, wait until the area is safe and then start treating the victims or drag them out of the area to the waiting paramedics.

The last item I'll cover with active shooter issues is prevention. Hundreds of shootings and terrorist attacks have been prevented by someone speaking up and saying something to the authorities about suspicious behavior. If you have employees or visitors who appear troubled or have made threats against the organization or its personnel,

153

report it to management and the police. Law Enforcement can look into the issue and see if there are any credible threats or in today's age, media postings. If nothing else they will have a list of people who have made threats in the past from which to start figuring out who might be involved should a shooting happen at your location.

Many active shooters were former employees, ex-spouses or clients who feel they've been wronged by the organization. Often these attacks come years after the initial incident and initially the people present have no idea who the person is or why the shooting took place.

The first shooting at Focus on the Family, a non-profit organization based out of Colorado Springs, shows how seemingly unconnected the active shooter can be from the organization and how people create a vendetta within their own mind against a church, school, company or individual.

Keven Dore walked into the front lobby of Focus on the Family and took a seat in a chair after throwing on the floor what appeared to be a bomb wired to a detonator held in one hand and a pistol in the other.[29] After the incident concluded it took law enforcement quite a while to figure out why Mr. Dore had attacked the organization.

As it turned out, Focus on the Family, at least in Dore's mind, was responsible for the destruction of his life. They were responsible for his loss of employment, physical disability, home foreclosure and his divorce which included losing the custody of his children. Keven Dore was there to make Focus on the Family pay for all they had done!

---

[29] Evil Invades Sanctuary by Carl Chinn

What connection did Focus have with Dore? Initially, investigators would say none; however, after weeks of probing a connection was finally made.

Keven Dore was basically a freelance construction worker. Many years prior to the incident, Dore had been working for a subcontractor to the general contractor during the construction of the new Focus on the Family building. Dore, disregarding all safety regulations, had been horsing around and decided to slide down one of the 30' metal beams to the main floor at the end of his shift. During this slide he lost control of the descent and upon reaching the bottom had impaled himself on a piece of rebar.

Workers compensation insurance paid for his medical expenses but, due to how the injury occurred, refused to pay him any permanent disability. He was physically unable to work, had no other skills and had no source of income so he eventually lost his home, wife and kids. His initial anger was at workers compensation, the general contractor and the subcontractor. When his legal attempts to get them to pay for his disability failed, he turned his anger towards the client, Focus on the Family which eventually resulted in the attack.

I bring this up to show that an active shooter walking through the front door of any facility can happen to anyone, at any time, for any number of reasons. Some grievances may be real as in the case of a terminated employee or ex-spouse and some, as in this case, can be totally created within the deranged mind of the assailant or, as in numerous recent terrorist attacks, the victims were simply in the wrong place at the wrong time. Nobody is 100% immune to this threat and in today's world everyone should be prepared to react properly should it happen.

The three steps outlined in this chapter work no matter where you are, work, school, church, the mall, anywhere. Please remember Run, Hide, Fight and do not hesitate should an active shooter event take place.

10

Foreign Travel

Now that your eyes have been opened to the dangers one may possibly face on any given day both at home and abroad, let's move on and address issues specific to travel into a foreign country. I love traveling to foreign countries. The topography, the architecture, the people, the culture, and in most cases the food are a wonderful diversion from the American way of life. The cultural differences are wonderful to take in and enjoy; however, we must remember that life in other countries is not quite like life is here in the good old U.S.A.

Even though things appear very safe and secure on the surface, take a closer look at the details in the daily lives of people in each country you visit. Do all the businesses and homes have bars on their windows? In residential neighborhoods do the houses all have 10-foot-high concrete walls around the back yard with concertina wire or glass shards imbedded around the top? Do the shops close their doors every day at 5 o'clock and everyone heads home to the secure sanctuary of their protected residences or, on the flip side, do the businesses and restaurants stay open late at night with people milling about the streets long after dark?

In law enforcement we call these things clues, items that provide you with a good idea of what the security threats are like in the area. The people who live there have learned over generations how to live and be safe without even giving it a second thought. The best rule of thumb is to follow the lead of the local population and then add an additional layer of security to your daily life while traveling in their country. Remember, you're not as attuned to the local dangers as they are.

My friend Chris, who is the president of an international construction ministry, and I were sitting on the back porch one evening talking about this subject when he told me the story about how he and his family learned the hard way about following the locals' security habits, even when you don't see any dangers. Chris and his family had been working in Ecuador for several years building a major educational facility. They had observed how the little town where they lived rolled up the sidewalks every day at 5 o'clock and how all the houses built huge concrete walls around their property even before a new house went up, but they never fully grasped the concept of why. Security threats were never really talked about with the local populous. It was simply a way of life for them and the locals assumed everyone knew what to do in order to keep themselves safe; however, Chris missed the clues.

They built their facility just outside of town. They lived in an apartment attached to the main building and, being Americas, they never considered acquiring funding to build a security wall around the property. That is until one fateful evening when everything changed.

Just after dinner, around 6 o'clock, the door suddenly burst open and a team of armed men stormed inside their tiny apartment. Chris, his wife and son were tied up and held at gun point while these men systematically robbed them of everything they owned. They even stripped the car right down to the frame and left it sitting on blocks. They intended to take Chris as a hostage for ransom; however, this plan changed due to a great job of acting. Chris was able to fake a heart attack so well over the 3 to 4-hour ordeal that his assailants, who I believe from Chris' description were either former FARC (Federal Armed Revolutionary of Columbia) soldiers or possibly a rogue band of current FARC militia, including one who had some level of medical training, fully believed Chris was suffering a heart attack. They thought that Chris might die in the process of kidnapping him so they left him behind as they departed. Now he understands why the locals close their shops and build security fences around their homes. They left Chris and his family with nothing, absolutely nothing! This brings us to my next piece of advice for foreign travel.

In the early stages of this book I talked about making pre-travel preparations and several specific items to leave behind, one being a copy of your itinerary. For foreign travel you need to take that process one step further. Before you travel overseas you need to make 3 color copies of your travel documents (the itinerary can be black and white). This needs to include a copy of your travel itinerary, (airline, hotel, local lodging, ground travel plans,) a color copy of your passport (specifically the picture page with your personal identification information) and your driver's license.

One copy of these documents needs to be with you at all times. In fact, I like to keep these with me when traveling around in a foreign country and keep the other copies along with the original documents safe back at the hotel. If you've renewed your passport and driver's license, keep the old ones (the state department punches a hole in your old passport) and carry these as you travel around town while keeping the current versions safe back at your hotel.

One copy of these documents needs to be secured either in your room safe, with the trip supervisor or locked up safely with your money and other important items in a hotel safety deposit box (my preferred location). This way, if the travel documents you have with you get stolen, you have the basics needed to get home back at the hotel in the safe.

The third copy needs to be left at home with someone you trust like your spouse, a family member or with your employer. Should something happen to the point that you are not able to take care of things on your own (let's consider a major medical issue, the earthquake in Haiti, a kidnapping, etc.), someone back in the US has the basic documents they need to take to the nearest US Department of State office so that they can provide you with a set of the temporary travel documents needed to get home. The color copies of these documents, vs. black and white, will show some of the security details in the documents that will help the State Department verify their authenticity.

In addition to hard copies of these documents I also like to scan and email a copy of these documents to myself. Internet cafés are available in most major cities and in many hotels where, if needed, I can access a computer, log into my email account and retrieve the scanned copies of my travel documents. These can also be emailed to the State Department to speed up the process of getting you home.

Before leaving on a trip to some foreign location, many people ask, "What vaccinations or medications do I need?" That really depends on where you are going. Both, the World Health Organization and the CDC, are good places to start looking for information on these medical issues. They provide a wealth of country specific information on their websites.

Another good place to turn is a medical travel clinic. There are travel clinics in just about every mid-sized city in the US and they can tell you exactly what vaccinations or medications are required or recommended for the countries you plan to visit. It used to be that certain vaccinations were required before traveling to many countries but today most countries only recommend these protective measures. In most situations it's up to the traveler to decide whether the risks justify the side effects of the medications.

One thing to keep in mind is that, as Americans, our immune systems are one of the weakest in the world. We eat clean food, our water is purified and many parents don't even let their kids get dirty anymore. This causes our immune systems to not be as strong as people in many foreign countries who have battled a constant barrage of viruses, bacteria and infections from birth which actually strengthens their immune system. People in foreign countries are able to drink the water without getting sick, whereas that same water will instantly make us sick! Americans need to take extra precautions to avoid and prevent those invasive bacteria, viruses and infections from making us sick and ruining a great trip.

While I'm on the topic of medical issues, have you considered calling your insurance carrier to ask whether they provide coverage for the country you intend to visit? Some do, some may only provide coverage in a limited number of specific countries and many do not provide any coverage outside the US. It's good to know ahead of time what you may have to deal with. Medical facilities in many countries will only accept cash from foreign tourists even if they do have valid medical insurance. They often require a financial deposit before treating the issue and won't release a patient from their care until either the patient, or his insurance company, have paid the bill in full.

Travel insurance is something that might be worth considering. In general, travel insurance is fairly cheap, especially if you plan to make a number of trips each year. A couple of hundred dollars will generally cover a married couple for a year. Many churches purchase group coverage for their mission teams which can generally save some money.

If you decide to purchase travel insurance, there are a couple of items you need to look for in the policy. When looking into travel insurance, make sure the policy includes medical evacuations and political evacuations. Policies with and without these two items generally run about the same price, so make sure yours has these in it. The medical evacuation clause covers the expenses to get you out of the country and into a location where proper medical care can be obtain should you become seriously ill or injured. The political evacuation clause covers the expenses when Americans are suddenly evacuated out of a country for security reasons like a coup, or if a war breaks out, like what happened in Egypt in 2001, in Lebanon in 2006 and Yemen in 2015. If the price of the policy is the same, it only makes sense to get what you may need.

Speaking of insurance, many wealthy Americans travel overseas and never consider the issue that in many countries their life insurance policies are null and void. Most, if not all life insurance policies will not pay if you travel to a country that has an active State Department travel warning. Places like Israel are visited by tens of thousands of Americans each year and parts of Israel have had an active travel warning for decades. Should you die during a trip to these areas, your family generally won't receive a dime from your life insurance policy.[30] Not that this will keep you from going on your trip but it might be a good idea, just like with your medical insurance carrier, to call and ask before you go just so you'll know what your policy does and does not cover.

There are several reasons why travelers run into problems in foreign countries. Many of these issues could have been prevented had the travelers just taken the time to do a little research before they left home to discover what the current threats were to their safety in the region or even the specific town they planned to visit.

The number one reason people get into trouble overseas is that they never do this research. The second is that when they do complete the research, people ignore the information. Whether it is an official travel warning from the State Department or small local issues, Americans tend to believe that "it won't happen to me."

When you find specific security-related issues, pay attention to them and consider adjusting your travels to avoid placing yourself where these issues could be a problem. Here is a simple example. I was teaching a travel safety seminar for a group of people who were headed to Guatemala. During a break I was approached and asked about a specific town, so I simply did a quick internet search on robberies of tourists and the town name. What I found was a report stating that American women had been getting their purses stolen repeatedly at one of the local beaches and in one of the local markets. My simple recommendation to the group on avoiding this known security issue was to have the women leave their purses in

---

[30] www.jrcinsurancegroup.com/life-insurance-for-world-traveller/

the hotel and have the men carry their money and personal identification when traveling to these two areas. It can be that simple, adjusting your activities to avoid a known threat.

When traveling with groups of 3 people or more, I like to ask each person to independently research the travel issues for where we plan to visit. People doing independent research tend to come up with different information. By getting together and comparing all of the information as a traveling group, everyone can be made aware of the threats and decide whether there is a need to adjust the itinerary or maybe just the local travel habits to avoid these dangers. As I mentioned above, if someone finds on a search engine that there have been a rash of purse thefts on the local beach in the town we plan to visit, make sure the women leave their purses locked away in the hotel room and have the men carry their belongings when we go to the beach.

The third reason people get into serious trouble overseas is that they do not have a viable emergency action plan. Should a major disaster happen during your travels, like the earthquake in Haiti, do you have an emergency action plan that includes several contingencies and has everyone in the group reviewed and understood the plan?

Most people who travel overseas never even consider making an emergency action plan. Even those traveling in groups fail to have a plan at all other than, "We'll meet in the hotel lobby if something goes wrong." That is not an emergency plan and it does not include any sort of back-up. If you are traveling in a group you need to have a *written* emergency action plan and everyone in the party needs to have a copy.

An emergency action plan needs to include at least the following information for everyone in the group:

- Name of each traveler and travel itinerary
- Emergency contact information for everyone
- Primary meeting place if something goes wrong
- Secondary meeting place if you can't get to the primary
- Nearest Embassy or Consulate (may be the Canadian, British or Australian if there is no US Embassy)
- Nearest safe country if you have to leave this one and where you should meet (embassy or airport)
- The address of your hotel and the nearest embassy written in the local language that you can hand to a cab driver who can read it and take you there
- A map (Google Earth or Bing maps work well) showing the major roads, location of your hotel, secondary meeting place, embassy, police station and hospital
- A second map showing the route to take to the nearest safe country

There are lots of items that can be included in an emergency action plan but these are the minimum. Let's take a look at a couple of examples of why you need to have this information on you at all times and why everyone in your party needs to have it.

In 2008 Martin was asked to speak at a conference in Mumbai, India. He decided to take his 15-year-old daughter Gloria with him for the cultural experience. The group he was speaking to flew them both into the country and put them up at the nicest place in town, the Taj Mahal Hotel. This was the equivalent of India's Ritz Carlton hotel in New York.

After checking into their room, Martin decided to take a shower and relax while his daughter, full of excitement on her first trip outside the US, grabbed her swimming suit and headed for the pool. Fifteen minutes later they both heard explosions followed by rounds of AK47 automatic gunfire, yelling and screaming.

Now this story goes in two directions. Gloria realizes very quickly that something is seriously wrong. She sees the smoke rising from the lobby so she grabs her bag and towel, heads out the back gate from the pool, travels down a hallway to reach a service exit and leaves the hotel through the employee parking lot (active shooter rule number 1: Run. If you can get out, get out!)

For a full day Gloria wandered back and forth a block away behind the police barricades, waiting for news on her father, cold and hungry. Eventually a local family noticed her plight, took her into their home and provided her with some food and clothing.

Meanwhile Martin is jolted awake from his nap by the same explosions and gunfire. He takes just a moment to look outside his hotel room door and sees the gunmen coming down the hall, systematically kicking in the door to each room calling out specifically for American and British guests. Thinking quickly, Martin throws the covers up on his bed to make it look as though nobody had slept in it. He turns off all the lights in the room, crawls under the sink in the bathroom and then drapes a large towel over his body in an effort to hide (Active shooter Rule number 2: If you can't get out - Hide.)

Within 30 seconds the door is kicked open by the gunmen who storm into the room and turn on the lights. Seeing the empty beds and assuming that the room is empty, they leave and continue down the hallway specifically looking for more Americans and Brit's to take hostage.

Martin remained under that sink for four days until November 29th when the event ended. During this time Martin was sure that Gloria had been killed at the pool and in turn, Gloria was certain that her father had been either kidnapped or killed in his room. It wasn't until two days after the terrorists had been captured and the remaining hotel guests were allowed to walk out of the hotel that the two finally met and realized they were both fine. They inadvertently ran into each other at a location where photographs of the victims were being displayed for families to identify the bodies. You can only imagine their relief as they found each other alive.

Their emergency action plan had been to simply meet in the lobby of the hotel should anything happen during their trip. Of course that was impossible and they had never even considered having a secondary location to go to. Had they had a proper emergency action plan, Gloria would have been at their secondary location waiting for her father who would have gone directly to that secondary location as soon as he was able to leave the hotel. That would have saved them days of pain and the grief of looking through horrendous photos trying to identify their loved one from the pictures of the 164 people who were killed and another 308 that were seriously injured.

Thousands of Americans found out the hard way about not only having a primary and a secondary meeting place, but also having a third location in the nearest safe country along with a map showing how to get there during the January 12, 2010 earthquake in Port au Prince, Haiti.

In most cases there was no hotel to return to. The embassy was destroyed and there were no flights leaving the country. Hundreds of Americans in Haiti had to make their way through the countryside to Santa Domingo in the Dominican Republic to get home but few knew how to get there. Most people who made that trip never considered that they would encounter snow-capped mountains when visiting a Caribbean Island or that major roads between the capitals of Haiti and the Dominican Republic were few and far between and nothing like what Americans would consider a major highway.

So, when you and your group are making plans to visit a foreign country, spend a little time getting to know the area and the security threats specific to the cities you'll be visiting and put together a good emergency action plan.

So, where do you find good, reliable information on security-related issues for a foreign country? The following are sources of information where you can find the majority of information that you will need:

I usually start my research by visiting the US Department of State website at www.Travel.State.gov. There you will find the official government travel warnings along with specific embassy guidance for foreign travelers. The guidance is usually general in nature for the whole country but will give you a good idea of what problems exist.

The second place I look is a commercial site that provides specific security-related information on countries all over the world. Stratfor, www.Stratfor.com, is the leader in global intelligence in the commercial sector. Although much of their information must be obtained by paying a small annual fee (which may be worth the cost for the church), Stratfor offers a lot of information for free. They also allow you to sign up for a trial use of their site to include email alerts on security issues as they happen. If you truly want to get an idea about what happens around the world with real-time information, pay for a Stratfor subscription and you'll be shocked at what takes place virtually each and every day.

Another good government site is **www.OSAC.gov**. This is the Overseas Advisory Council and they often provide access to a number of security-related issues. **www.FBI.gov** is another location that provides information on various countries that you might find useful.

All of these websites are good for gaining an overall idea of the security threats that exist for a country. I also like to simply utilize a search engine, like Google or Bing, where you can search for issues that have arisen in the particular cities that you will be visiting. You can often find very specific information not listed on the government sites.

Of course, the best source of information comes from someone who is there, on the ground and has been there for several years; a local is the best source of information. He or she will know better than anyone what the security threats are in the local area, the city or even the specific neighborhood you'll be visiting. Use the government sites to get an overall picture of the situation. Try to get as much specific local information as possible and combine that information with what you see and the information you get from a local source.

Regardless of how much information you acquire, none of it does any good if you ignore it. Take the information seriously and decide if you should change what you're doing or where you are going. Above all, keep your eyes open to what is happening around you at all times. You are your best security defense against getting into trouble!

Researching a country will not only make your trip safer but it will also make your trip much more enjoyable. You'll not only learn about the security issues but you'll learn more and more about the country, the culture and its people. The more you know and understand, the more you'll enjoy the trip and the more effective you'll be in your cross cultural transactions.

As you are doing your research, here are some specific items that you should look for. You need to look into the demographics of the region. What is the major religion in the area? On that note, we spoke a few minutes ago about Haiti. What is the major religion in Haiti? Many Americans would say Catholicism but in actuality it's Voodoo. Every president of the country has followed Voodoo for as long as anyone can remember and that culture is *VERY* different from ours!

When you are traveling to a country with a culture that is considerably different from your own, you need to have a basic understanding of what it is like. What are some of the customs or superstitions? Are there things that Americans do that may offend people in that country?

Most Americans traveling on mission trips are geared 100% toward completing the mission they set out to accomplish. As an example, let's say your group is going into a country to dig a well to provide the town with fresh drinking water. You will work effortlessly from dawn to dusk to get that well dug and if you don't get it finished, many will consider the trip as a failure. On the other hand, the locals in that village have never had a well. They've always carried water from the river up to the village and life hasn't changed just because you didn't get the well dug. If you didn't finish it, the next group will or may. For you the trip was a failure because the well was not completed but for the local villagers the trip was a failure, not because the well didn't get completed but because those rude Americans came to their village and all they wanted to do was dig in the dirt. They never took the time to get to know the villagers.

In many cultures getting to know someone is much more important than digging a well or raising a new building. In their culture, if you had spent a few hours, even a full day getting to know them and their families, regardless of what you did or did not accomplish, the trip would have been a huge success in their eyes. So take a little time and research the culture before you head out on your trip.

From a security standpoint you need to take a good look during your research at the current and past political stability of the country and any political concerns. Has there been a history of coups? Are tensions between the location you plan to travel and a neighboring country on edge? Are there Rebel groups that might invade or could a war break out? These items need to be researched and added into your security plans. If instability or tensions and war are a possibility, then attention needs to be paid to those situations not only by yourself while in the country but also monitored by people back home who may have better access to the news and internet than you do.

What is the organized crime situation in the country? Mexico immediately comes to mind. That country has changed tremendously since the turn of the century. Mexico used to be a wonderful place to visit and parts of the country still are but in other parts, not just along the border, the drug cartels have basically turned the country into an active war zone without any perceivable law enforcement. Over 56,000 people have been murdered in specific parts of Mexico over the past 10 years.[31]

Just like in Mexico, countries change and not always for the worse. Take Columbia, for example. In the 1970s Columbia was a beautiful place to visit but with the growth of the FARC, security threats to American citizens grew worse and worse through the 80s and 90s to where the country was no longer a safe place to visit or do business. Then, after 2000 the country began to stabilize and in 2015 the Columbian government started open peace negotiations with the FARC. Columbia is once again a very beautiful location in which to work and security is getting much better. Of course, that depends on where in Columbia you plan to go. The FARC still controls a vast portion of the southern half of the country and the FARC is very anti-American. That's where doing your homework for any country you plan to visit pays off. Knowing where you can/should go and knowing where you shouldn't is very important.

Just like the FARC in Columbia, every country, even the US, has terrorist issues. In many countries terrorist activity will be active enough that you'll need to research which parts of the country are safe and which parts are not. Take the Philippines, for instance. Thousands of Americans travel safely to the Philippines each year but these travelers

---

[31] www.unodc.org

usually avoid the southern islands where the Abu Sayyaf, an Islamic terror group closely associated with al-Quaeda, controls much of the country.

As discussed previously, during your pre-travel research you need to locate the safe houses: the embassy, consulate, local police station, hospitals, malls, etc. These should be included on the map with written addresses as part of your emergency action plan.

As with the island of Hispaniola, where a major mountain range separates Haiti from the Dominican Republic, you should also become familiar with the geography of the country as well as surrounding countries. Which neighboring countries are safe and welcome Americans and which ones do not?

Take a look at Ecuador and Israel, for example. If you had to make your way out of either of these countries during an emergency situation, which way would you go? Would you go north, south, east or west?

In Ecuador, if you travel north and get off the major Pan American Highway, you very well may end up in FARC controlled territory. In Israel would you want to travel north into Lebanon or east into Jordan? Depending on where in the country you were when things turned bad, with whom and for what reason, you may or may not want to cross the West Bank into Jordan. Knowing the geography ahead of time will help you make these critical security-related decisions should the time ever arise. You may say, "Nothing like that will ever happen." So did many Americans working in Port au Prince! Having to evacuate to the Dominican Republic was probably the last thing they considered when making travel plans.

When it comes to studying the region for familiarization there is a lot more you want to learn about the country and/or local area other than just the security threats. Take time to study the history of the country or even the history of the specific area where you'll be traveling. People coming to America have it easy in this regard as we've only been around a couple of hundred years but many of the countries you'll travel to consider America a fledgling country. As compared to our 200 years, their history may go back thousands of years.

Study their local customs so you understand what it is you're looking at when you see them. Study their lifestyles, religion and superstitions. Simple gestures such as pointing at your chest, wiping your hand across your chest or showing someone the bottom of your shoe are considered extremely offensive in other cultures. Things you never considered and did, never intending to offend anyone, can quickly destroy a good relationship.

Take a little time and try to learn a few simple phrases in the local language. Even if you can't get the right words to come out, just the fact that you are trying to speak their language will show the local people that you care and they will be much more willing to help you.

One item I've carried in countries where I didn't speak the language is the Kwikpoint International Travel Translator which is a very simple solution that overcomes language barriers. The International Travel Translator is a weather resistant fold-out card that includes multiple categories of pictures. You simply point to the picture of what you want, require or where you need directions to and anyone will understand what you mean regardless of language.

Have you taken the time to look into the weather conditions at the time of year you plan to visit the country? South Africa and the lower half of South America come to mind. Many people travel down there in our summer only to discover daily high temperatures in the 20s and 30s. Yes, it is winter south of the equator between May and August, so you had better take a jacket! Are you visiting during the monsoon season? In many countries it rains all day, every day for months on end during the monsoon season. Find out what the predominant weather patterns are going to be so you can take clothing appropriate to the climate and conditions you can expect to encounter.

I have stated repeatedly about needing to learn about the local culture but I really can't stress this issue enough. Cultural differences, not just with the people you'll be working with but also those in the surrounding countryside, may be tremendously different from ours. How sad is the day when one of your children dies by committing suicide? It's hard for any American to truly comprehend that a mother's proudest moment in life is when her teenage son or daughter commits suicide, blows himself or herself up with a body bomb and kills 30 or 40 of those infidel Americans in the process. In some of the radicalized Islamic cultures, that is exactly how they think.

Yes, this is an extreme example but it's a true example of how differently people think in other countries. Cultural differences can be as extreme as this or as simple as an offensive hand gesture or a single word spoken in the wrong context. Once you understand the cultural differences for the entire region you plan to visit, then you can avoid inadvertently offending someone and possibly placing yourself in harm's way.

Regarding cultural differences, I'd like to spend a few moments discussing the differences between the American or Western culture and the Arab culture. When it comes to the Arab culture most Americans have a hard time understanding why Arabs do some of the things they do. With the volume of trips conducted in Arab countries, understanding a few basic cultural differences may help you relate to the people you'll meet and work with.

Unlike Muslims who can be from any country or any ethnic background, Arabs come from a particular part of the world. Do you think all Arabs are Muslims? No, Arabs can actually be from any religion and in fact many Arabs are Christians. Arabs are those guys who wear turbans, right? Wrong. Some Arabs do wear a headdress but most people who wear turbans are Sikhs from India. They are not Arabs nor are they Muslims.

There are some unique cultural or philosophical differences between Westerners and Arabs that people traveling to Arab countries should try to comprehend as they can have a huge impact in your personal relations. Let's look at a few of these differences:

Westerners tend to take ownership of their guilty deeds and admit their mistakes so that they may be forgiven. In an Arab culture it's better to blame others for your guilty deeds in order to avoid being shamed. Shame is to be avoided at all costs. This includes any shame to you or to your family name!

Westerners feel that it's better to tell the truth and admit their faults in order to correct problems they have caused. Arabs feel that it is better to deny the truth, even when the truth is obvious, in order to preserve "face."

Westerners normally respond rationally when presented with the facts. Rules are made for a reason and should not be broken (not that any of us have ever broken a rule or two.) In the Arab culture, they perceive maintaining a person's honor as much more important than any facts. Their solution to resolving an issue may be to reinterpret the facts to suit their needs. People and honor are much more important than any facts, so if the facts cause disgrace to a person, they will change the facts.

For Westerners status is gained through their actions and is earned through their good deeds. For Arabs status is gained through birth, and no matter what they do, their status in life will never change. To help understand this, consider who rules a western country (an elected president) and who rules an Arab country (the King.)

Westerners believe that they control their environment but for an Arab, Allah is in control and nothing you do will change the outcome.

Quite often it's very hard for Americans to grasp these cultural differences. Our lives, from the time we are born to the present day, are built around much different values and philosophies. The way we think is based upon our cultural values. The same can be said from their point of view. Arabs have a very hard time understanding why Americans act the way they do. They feel we are arrogant, rude and uncivilized people because of these cultural differences, but if you understand some of these basic concepts it will help you to better work with these people and avoid causing the many hard feelings that have developed between these two cultures. It may also help prevent many of the security-related issues that can happen when traveling into foreign countries.

Lots of things can go wrong when traveling overseas. Much of it can be unavoidable, like getting sick or injured. I can assure you that all of the Americans working in Haiti when the earthquake hit had never considered an earthquake as even a remote possibility but just like it did in Haiti, things can go wrong. I have traveled into a foreign country thinking that everything was safe and secure only to walk around the corner of my hotel and straight into the path of a huge civil uprising such as in Caracas where I accidentally ran into a demonstration against President Chaves. Fortunately, I had studied the travel warnings and researched the Embassy guidance and knew that an election was in progress. The State Department Travel Warnings stated that violent protests were possible; I just never thought that I'd actually walk into the middle of a major demonstration which, within seconds, turned into a full-scale riot between the demonstrators and the federal police.

When conducting your pre-travel research, pay attention to any specific guidance posted by the embassy. The embassy posted the following guidance on their website prior to the 2010 earthquake in Haiti: *"US Embassy personnel are under a curfew. All embassy personnel and their family members must be off the streets and secured in resident housing by 5 p.m. each day."*

So, if I were leading a team into Haiti or any other country and found a statement like this, requiring all government personnel and their families to be off the streets and secure by 5 p.m., I can assure you my mission team would be off the streets and secure by 4:30!

The embassy guidance also stated: "The Department of State strongly advises US citizens traveling to Haiti to register their travels online at travelregistration.state.gov or with the Consular Section of the US Embassy in Port-au-Prince."

If you are not registering your foreign travels with the State Department, you need to start right now! Registration is made through the Smart Traveler Enrollment Program at:

https://step.state.gov/step/

Registering your trip only takes a few minutes and it's free. The information listed in the example of the Emergency Action Plan included in the appendix of this book will have all the information needed to complete the registration. In addition to yourself, you can add all of your traveling companions at the same time in just a few additional steps. Registering your trip allows the State Department to locate you during an emergency or an evacuation. If you don't register, they don't know you're in the country and will never come looking for you.

The State Department used this registration data to go look for the college students in Granada, business executives in Egypt and Lebanon and the non-governmental organizations working in Haiti during the earthquake. Hundreds or even thousands of Americans were in the country during these security events but the government never came to their rescue because they had not registered their travels.

Another issue to consider is the legal problems that can arise when traveling in a foreign country. Laws in foreign countries can be very different than they are here in the US and often there are many myths out there that some things are legal when they are not. Illegal drugs are a good example. Many Americans think that marijuana is legal in places like Jamaica or Canada where it actually is illegal. The last place you want a member of your party to end up is in the local jail of some foreign country! Do you remember the 10 Baptist missionaries from Idaho who were arrested and thrown into a Haitian jail after the earthquake while trying to take 33 children across the border into the Dominican Republic?[32] Laura Silsby was the last of these people to be released after spending 3 months and 8 days in a Haitian jail, a place none of us ever want to be.

I've seen something as simple as taking pictures of the wrong place or the wrong people get Americans into major trouble in foreign countries, and some have even been jailed or killed for what we would think were very harmless actions. Prior to 2015, just about everyone who had traveled to England on vacation has taken pictures of the changing of the guards at Buckingham Palace. Here in America it seems like the first thing that happens during a police officer's daily job is for someone to pull out a cell phone and start recording, but if you take a picture of a policeman in Columbia, Mexico and many other foreign countries, it is a felony criminal offense and you could spend your entire trip sitting in a local jail cell. You have to understand this from their security point of view. As an example, cartels will take pictures of the police officers they intend to get rid of before they send their hit team out to take care of the job. Taking pictures of police officers or government buildings is never a good idea when you are away from home.

Another problem I've seen Americans get into trouble for is buying those interesting little antique pottery pieces and statues sold in the local markets. These pieces are often dug up and stolen from old gravesites and then sold for

[32] www.cnn.com/2010/CRIME/05/17/haiti.silsby.freed/

huge profits to the tourists. Governments consider these items national treasures and countless Americans have been fined and even arrested when clearing Customs trying to bring these items home. It even happens here in the US where grave robbers dig up artifacts from the Native American burial sites and sell them on the black market. Stay away from ANY antiques and only bring home newly made items.

In a previous chapter I talked about why Americans make such good targets for the local criminal elements. You probably don't speak the language, you probably don't know how to call the police and even if they are caught and arrested, you won't be there to testify against the criminals when their case goes to trial. Knowing that these issues make us a preferred target, you need to think about how obviously you stand out in a crowd as an American.

You can usually spot an American in a foreign country 100 feet away. The clothing and shoes they wear, the jewelry on American women, their language, mannerisms and sometimes their arrogant attitude make it quite obvious to locals that these people are from the U.S.A. When you're traveling in a foreign country, try to dress down as much as possible. It's best to wear plain, darker colored clothes without any big American logos. Traveling overseas is not the time to wear your Dallas Cowboys, Atlanta Falcons, or I ♥ NYC shirt!

One of the surprising things I've found in my travels is that there are blond-haired, blue-eyed Germans living in just about every country of the world. These people of German descent moved into these countries during or shortly after World War II and are now natives of that country. Although they may look like many Americans with pale skin, blond hair and blue eyes, they don't dress like Americans; they dress like the locals. You should try to do the same and blend into the country as much as possible.

I try to take a good look at these Caucasian locals and attempt to dress as close as possible to how they dress; and if I'm wearing anything that seems to be bringing a lot of attention to myself, I put it away and I don't wear it again.

One summer a few years back, I was on vacation with my family and got called to the interior of Brazil for a mission. I didn't have time to go home and pack so I left from where I was and flew straight down to South America. Being on a western mountain vacation, the only shoes I had with me were heavy hiking boots. Between stepping off the airplane in Sao Paulo to arriving at my hotel I noticed six people point at my hiking boots. Nobody in Brazil wore heavy boots like that. All the men wore these thin, flat leather dress shoes, even with jeans and a T-shirt, where Americans would normally wear athletic shoes.

My hiking boots were drawing a tremendous amount of attention to me, so as soon as I got checked into the hotel, I walked to the mall across the street and bought a pair of flat leather shoes like all of the local Caucasian men were wearing. From that moment on not a single person paid any attention to a blue-eyed, fair-haired American traveling in a foreign country. At 6'2" with blond hair, blue eyes and sporting a new pair of flat leather shoes, I looked like all the other locals of German decent who lived there.

Are your hiking boots, hat, shirt, backpack, purse or jewelry drawing attention? It doesn't matter what the item is, if something you have or something you are doing is bringing a lot of attention to you from the locals, it will bring a lot of attention to you from the criminal element as well. Get rid of that item or activity, pack it away or stop doing it until you get home and try to blend in. When criminals are choosing their next American target this will lessen the chances that it will be you.

Americans have a number of misconceptions about traveling in foreign countries. Most Americans believe that they will be safe wherever they go, walking blindly into harm's way. Most Americans believe that we'll be welcome wherever we go.

Working as a pilot with access to HF and UHF military radio systems, flying at altitude late at night, I used to enjoy tuning in radio stations in various foreign countries just to listen to the news. You gain a new perspective on how Americans are perceived in the world when you listen to their news reports. We are the 900-pound gorillas who like to flex our muscles around the world. A lot of countries, in fact most of the world's countries don't particularly like Americans, at least not the way we think we're liked. Most Americans think that, because our country sends humanitarian aid and comes over with our military to free the oppressed, that we'll be loved and appreciated wherever we go. It's just not so! This is one of the biggest reasons why America and Americans are the chosen targets for terrorist organizations.

11

Introduction to Terrorism

"Somewhere a *'True Believer'* is training to kill you! He is training with minimum food or water, in austere conditions both day and night. The only thing clean on him is his weapon. He doesn't worry about what workout to do. His rucksack weighs what it weighs, and he runs until the enemy stops chasing him. The *'True Believer'* doesn't care how hard it is, he only knows that he either wins or he dies. He doesn't go home at 5 o'clock; he IS home. He knows only *"**the Cause**."*

This speech is read during the welcoming statements at the Army Special Forces Assessment and Selection Course. It probably gives one of the best insights into the mindset of terrorist organizations that I've ever heard or read. Terrorist organizations are so ingrained into *"the Cause,"* their cause, whatever that may be, that all other thoughts or actions become secondary.

In this chapter you will be provided with a basic understanding of terrorism and the terrorist issues that may affect your travels. Although terrorists span every ethnic and religious group in the world, including the Christian faith here in America and abroad, I will also try to provide a basic understanding of the Islamic faith because most Americans have no comprehension of the religion of Islam, Muslims or the different divisions within the faith.

How many countries have terrorist organizations actively operating within their borders? Answer: all of them.

Every country in the world has active terrorist organizations operating inside their borders including right here at home. America has as many, if not more terrorist organizations working within our borders as any other country in the world. Here at home we have everything from al-Qaeda to radical Nazi skinheads conducting terrorist operations around the country and many of them do much of it openly within the law. In fact the September 11th hijackers committed no crime, including taking those box cutters onboard the aircraft, until they got out of their seats during flight and took the first flight attendant hostage. At that time it was legal to take box cutters and small pocket knives past security screening and onboard a commercial airline flight.

Even though a fair amount of terrorist-related events happen right here in America, much of this activity is generally hidden from the American public. Over the past couple of decades, only about 50 of the more than 20,000 attempted terrorist attacks in the US have been reported in the news with more than a brief mention. Pay attention to the news for a while and see how many terrorist-related items you notice. A cell was taken down by police in some city or an attempted bombing was foiled by the FBI during an undercover sting. The news media will usually only mention these types of events once or twice before pulling them off the air. In fact, you'll notice some of these events being talked about in the morning and they won't even be mentioned during the evening news broadcasts.

Here is an example: Do you remember the car bomb that went off in Times Square in New York City? Very few people do. If not, conduct an internet search on any search engine image page and read the articles on the web.[33] You'll find the actual pictures of the bomb explosion caught on security cameras in Times Square. Had the

---

[33] www.nytimes.com/2010/05/02/nyregion/02timessquare.html?pagewanted=all&_r=0

bomb not malfunctioned and exploded a couple of hours earlier than planned, hundreds of people heading to Wall Street would have been victims; yet this terrorist attack, in the heart of NYC, barely made the news that morning and was completely left out of the news broadcasts that evening.

Once you start to pay attention to these stories you'll be amazed at how often this happens and for every one that you see there were dozens of terrorist-related events that you never heard about. If this is shocking to you regarding terrorist activity here at home, you can only imagine how many attempted terrorist attacks have taken place in foreign countries that we've never heard of.

The reason this issue is brought up is not to scare anyone out of taking an overseas trip. If that were the case, considering how many times terrorists have attempted to attack the US right here at home, you'd probably never leave your front yard. No, I bring it up only to make you pay attention to the information when you read something significant during your pre-travel research and, if necessary, change the way you and your traveling companions operate in a foreign country.

In general, Americans know virtually nothing about Muslims or the religion of Islam so I want to provide you with a little education on some of the basics of both so that the information you read during your pre-travel research makes sense. First, I'd like you to understand some of the terminology associated with this faith:

Islam is the religion that Muslims practice; however, there are two basic forms of Islam that I will discuss here in a moment.

A Muslim is "anyone" who follows the Islamic faith. It doesn't matter what nationality or ethnicity they are, anyone who follows the religion of Islam is a Muslim.

A Wahabbi is someone who follows the fundamentalist form of Islam. Wahabbi is basically a denomination of the Islamic faith. It would be the equivalent of a Christian telling you that they were a Baptist or Methodist.

A Salafi would be someone who follows the most puritanical, fundamentalist form of Islam. Terrorist groups like al-Qaeda are Salafis.

The word Jihad simply means *"finding the true path."* They believe that their actions are following the true path that leads to Allah (God). So a Salafi Jihadist would be a Muslim, practicing what he believes is the purest form of Islam and has taken it upon himself to live his life in such a way that everything he does is leading him closer to Allah.

Sharia is the traditional Islamic law which most Muslims follow. It is based upon the Quaran and teachings from Muhammad's life. Many Muslims reject the laws of the countries they live in and try to follow Sharia law instead.

So how many of these basic Islamic phrases have you heard before but never knew exactly what they meant? What about those Muslim names? They can be quite confusing to understand so let's take just a minute and break a couple of these down into their actual meaning.

We'll use Osama bin Laden's name as our first example.

Osama's full name was:
Osama bin Muhammad bin Awad bin Ladin.

- Osama is his name, the one he uses just like I use Brian when talking to other people.
- bin simply means "son of."
- Muhammad was Osama's father's name.
- Awad was his grandfather's name.
- Laden was his great grandfather and he chose to include his ancestral heritage back to his great grandfather because Laden was a great leader in the Islamic faith.

Reading through historical documents I often come across passages that reference a person's name followed by, "son of ___." I often wonder if the original text actually read: "Somebody bin ___."

Although many Muslims use their ancestral heritage in their name, depending on what country or even what part of a country they are from, many use descriptive words as part of their name. They use the term *al*-whatever, "al" being a descriptive name for something like their personal occupation or hometown. Let's take Osama's number two man in al-Qaeda as an example, Ayman al-Zawahiri.

His actual name was: Ayman Mohamed Rabi al-Zawahiri.

- Ayman was his name.
- Mohamed was his father's name.
- Rabi was his grandfather's name.
- Zawahiri is the small town in Saudi Arabia where he was from.

As part of the Islamic culture, Muslims often change the "bin" or "al" parts of their name at will. This can make things very difficult for law enforcement. Zawahiri also used the names, al-Hallaj, which means the cotton weaver because his family was in the textile industry and al-

189

Dukture, because he was also a doctor. Similarly, Muslims often change their lineage following the "bin" in their names. This can be confusing for people from western cultures but it's quite normal throughout the Arab culture.

Let's continue our basic understanding on this subject by discussing the different divisions within the Muslim faith.

Under the religion of Islam, there are two primary divisions in the faith, the Shia (or Shiite, Shiaa) which consists of approximately 15% of all Muslims and the Sunni which is the dominant portion comprising the other 85%.

To put this in common terms that most Americans can understand, this is the equivalent of having both Catholics and Protestants in the Christian faith. Under the Protestants you'd have the Baptists and Methodists (as in, under the Sunni you have the Wahabbi and Salafis.)

Here is the main difference between these two Islamic religions: The Shia follow leaders called Imams, who they believe are direct male descendants of Muhammad. This is much the same as the Kings and Queens in England and other European countries. You are born into the position as the religious leader.

The Sunni, on the other hand, believe that Mohammad did not have any male descendants so all of Mohammad's successors should be elected from the most qualified and trusted people called Caliphs. This is much the same as we have here in America. We elect by majority vote who we feel will be the best president.

It is this division in religious leadership ideology that has caused a huge split and great hatred within the Islamic faith. When you see the news reports from Iraq, most of the violence is Muslims against Muslims. Saddam Hussein and his ruling party were Shia even though they were not the majority. They held the money and the power in the country. Since the fall of Hussein the country has held elections and now the Sunnis are in power. It's this religious split in leadership ideology that has Muslims killing Muslims by the thousands.

It's under the Sunni that you find the Wahhabis, Salafis and of course your Salafi Jihadist terror groups. In conducting your pre-travel research it might be nice to know which version of Islam controls the country or, better yet, the region of the country you plan to visit. If nothing else, it may help prevent you from saying something that might offend one group or the other.

Of the world's 1.2 billion Muslims, only 1% are Salafi Jihadist. Of course that leaves about a million possible terrorists but not all Muslims following the True Path to Allah diverge into terrorist activities. There are lots of True Paths (Jihads) that do not lead to violence.

Here are some facts about Jihadists that I find interesting. Most are quite young, 26 being the average age. Most, approximately 55%, are middle class with 61% being college educated or having attended graduate school. Three fourths of Jihadists are professionals, like doctors or engineers and 73% are married.

What does the average terrorist look like? A young, well-educated, married man who is most probably working in a professional trade of some sort. This is not what most of us visualize when we think about a blood-thirsty terrorist whose only thought is how to kill as many Americans as possible. Take a look at the news reports. Nidal Hasan, an Army psychiatrist who killed 13 of his fellow soldiers at Fort Hood in 2009, fits the profile of the typical Salafi Jihadist Terrorist.[34]

Now before you start to think that all Muslims are bad, please understand that I am only describing a very small percentage of the Islamic faith and there are probably just as many Christian terrorists around the world. People like Timothy McVeigh and Terry Nichols who blew up the Murrah Federal Building in Oklahoma City.[35] They were just as dangerous as any Salafi Jihadist.

If you are traveling to, and working in, an Islamic country you need to do a little research into the religious control of the country. Before you arrive you should know who you may be encountering and how much tolerance they have for Westerners.

Most Americans don't approve of US law enforcement getting involved in major counter narcotics operations outside our country, but before you pass judgment on this issue, you must understand one major security point. Every, yes, every major terrorist organization in the world is primarily funded by the drug trade.

Al-Qaeda, for example, receives a major part of its financial funding from the opium/heroin trade. That also applies to the Abu Sayyaf in the Philippines. The FARC gets funding from the cocaine trade in Columbia, Ecuador and Peru. They may not be directly involved in growing or processing the drugs but they provide a safe haven for the growers, manufacturers and transporters of the narcotics.

---

[34] www.cbsnews.com/feature/tragedy-at-fort-hood/
[35] www.fbi.gov/about-us/history/famous-cases/oklahoma-city-bombing

In return they get a slice of the profits which helps fund their terrorist activities.

Every major terrorist organization in the world, with very few exceptions, has a vendetta against the United States. They simply don't like our freedoms or our culture. Our status in the world did not come from our birth rights; it was gained by a band of rouge immigrants who overthrew the imperialist British government to create a dominating world power. Of course, we feel a little different about the situation, but this view is most often how Americans are perceived throughout the rest of the world.

In just about every major terrorist organization there will be multiple different factions that break off and come up with their own agenda. We've often heard the terms, splinter groups or splinter cells, but few of us really understand what those terms mean. It goes without saying that major terrorist organizations pose a huge threat to our country, but it is often these smaller splinter groups or splinter cells that pose the biggest threat to the individual American traveling overseas.

Let's put these splinter cells into perspective by using American terms and looking at the Christian culture which most of us understand a little better. In the Christian culture, most churches have what is commonly called small groups or Bible study groups. These are very small groups of individuals who attend church services, usually at the same church, then meet in private to continue their religious educations in a private setting.

Splinter cells are much like our small groups. They attend religious services at the Mosque with everyone else and listen to the Imam speak about some topic like how they all need to stand up and take action in the name of Allah. The difference between these normal, everyday Islamic small groups and a terror cell is that some will take what the Imam said and twist it into thinking that they need to take some sort of terrorist-type action (a Jihad) to show their faith to Allah. This can also be done on a much larger scale when an entire sect (basically an entire church) heads off on some radical idea about taking action for Allah. We tend to call these larger groups a jihadist terrorist organization like al-Qaeda.

It's these smaller groups that can truly be a security issue for American travelers. They are so small, informal and working on their own that they tend to operate under the radar screen of international law enforcement or intelligence organizations.

Let's look at a hypothetical example of a splinter cell action. The group listens to the Imam who tells the congregation that they all need to stand up and take some sort of action to show their faith to Allah. This group meets in a private home three days later to discuss what the Imam meant by his words. During this process the group decides that they should go blow up a local hotel where all the Infidel Christians stay when they are in town in order to drive the infidels out of their country and prove their faith to Allah.

They then come to the realization that to take this action they need funding. They have to purchase the explosives, the detonators, pay the local bomb maker to build the device and then they'll need a truck to carry everything to the hotel. All of this will take money which they don't have, so how do they get the money to pay for everything? "I know," one of them says. "I know where there is a major building project taking place and the project is being managed by a couple of Americans. We'll kidnap one of the Americans while he's in route between the hotel and the job site and hold him for ransom. Once the ransom is paid we'll have all of the funding we need to build the bomb and truly show our faith to Allah through our actions."

This may sound a bit farfetched but this scenario has replayed itself over and over again in countless situations around the world. So now you see where you, as the American man or woman, could turn out to be a viable target for a terrorist. But before we move into kidnappings let's take a look at one last issue involving terrorist activities.

One of the common traits with terrorist activities that you need to look for when doing your pre-travel research, and in deciding what actions your group should change while operating in a particular country, involves significant dates. Terrorists tend to conduct activities repeatedly on the anniversary of certain dates, like the birthday of their leaders, the day their organization was dethroned from power, the day their leader was assassinated (Osama bin Laden or Saddam Hussein were both assassinated by Americans according to their text books). So when you are doing your research and come across any of these significant dates specific to the area you'll be working in, take a moment to consider what effect it could have on your travel plans. This might be the day you'll want to simply take a day off and relax at the hotel or go to work by a different route and avoid the local restaurants by calling for room service when you get back to your room.

I have an old friend who called me on April 17th many years ago and "told" me that we were going camping and turkey hunting that weekend with only two days' notice. Saturday evening, as we were sitting around the campfire, I asked him, "Why were you in such a rush and *insistent* that we come out here this weekend?" His answer kind of surprised me.

My friend was one of the ATF agents who had been shot on the roof of the Branch Davidian compound in Waco, Texas three years earlier. Exactly one year later he was working in the Murrah Building in Oklahoma City when Timothy McVeigh blew it up with a huge truck bomb in retaliation to the government's actions in Waco which was exactly one year previous on that day.[36] The way terrorist organizations operate, planning attacks on significant anniversaries and the way things tend to happen in threes, he didn't want to push his luck and felt the safest place he could be was as far away from everyone as he could get, out in the woods with me.

You should take this concept of noting the significant dates seriously and write them down when doing your research. If you travel to locations that have known safety threats from terrorist organizations and you come across some of these significant dates, pay attention and curtail your activities as much as possible on these days.

September 11th is a date that needs to be included in all of your security planning. The September 11th attacks on the World Trade Center buildings were the single most successful terrorist actions that have taken place in modern times. Terror cells around the world will continue for decades to come and will attempt to carry out future actions on this significant date.

---

[36] www.legacy.9news.com/story/news/local/2015/04/23/okc-bombing-luke-franey/26253625/

Do you recall the 2012 terrorist attack on the US Embassy in Libya that killed Ambassador Chris Stevens?[37]   What day did that attack take place? September 11th! The news media did not pick up on the date because the initial, but false, reports were that his death came from a rioting mob who was upset about an anti-Islamic video; however, as the truth came out, it became clear that this was a full-scale terrorist attack on a US Embassy and the assassination of an American Ambassador that was well planned and scheduled to take place on a very specific (significant) date, September 11th.

Terrorist organizations around the world are generally known for three major acts of terrorism: bombings, assassinations and kidnappings.   Americans traveling overseas are usually not going to be the targets of an assassination and there really isn't a whole lot you can do to prevent yourself from being hurt in a bombing situation; however, there is quite a bit you can do to prevent yourself from being taken hostage. Most of the information that I have already provided will help you in that area. There are, however, a few additions that I want to cover in the next chapter that are specific to how kidnappers choose their victims, how to identify when these things are taking place and what to do about them.

---

[37] www.en.wikipedia.org/wiki/2012_Benghazi_attack

12

Kidnappings

What are the chances that you will ever be taken hostage? Extremely low! Depending on where you travel, there is probably a greater chance that you'll be seriously injured by a coconut than be involved in a kidnapping. I'll repeat, this is dependent on where you travel! Kidnapping has become a full-time business in many countries and any book that gives the kind of specific details on international travel safety and security as I have needs to discuss this issue. Educating the reader on the possibility of being taken hostage, how to avoid it and, if it should happen, how to survive the situation must be addressed.

It used to be that kidnappings were pretty much targeted solely at corporate executives and missionary organizations involved in humanitarian relief work were fairly exempt; however, that has changed dramatically of the past few years. In 2013, Relief Web International published a special edition of the Aid Worker Security Report titled "The New Normal: Coping with the kidnapping threat."[38] In this security report Relief Web International stated that "Aid worker kidnappings have quadrupled over the past decade. Since 2009, more aid workers have been victims of kidnappings than of any other form of attack." With this change in selecting victims, nobody is safe from this threat.

Let's look at a few statistics on *reported* kidnappings, keeping in mind that only 10% of all kidnapping cases are ever reported to the authorities. This is most often due to fear that reporting the incident will trigger further

---

[38]

www.aidworkersecurity.org/sites/default/files/AidWorkerSecurityReport_2013_web.pdf kidnappings either to the family or to other mission teams. Most kidnappings are handled either by the family, the church, or through private hostage negotiation businesses and not through the law enforcement or the government agencies which track these statistics. So if you want to get a better idea on how huge a problem this is, you'd have to multiply the numbers by a factor of 9 or 10 to be anywhere close to the actual number of incidents.

In some countries kidnapping for profit really is a full-time commercial business. Spend some time in a modernized country like Brazil where they often talk openly about kidnapping incidents on the local news and you will walk away with a different perspective on this issue. In the large cities around Brazil, armed units of 30 to 50 men will take control of an entire apartment building to include any security personnel which just about every apartment and business employs. These armed criminal units go door to door until they find the right victim. They even go as far as hiring their own professional negotiators to ensure that they acquire the best ransom possible for their hostages.

Although the problem has gotten much better over the last decade in this country, let's take a look at the reported kidnapping numbers in Columbia during 2001. That year Amnesty International reported that Colombian authorities received reports of more than 300 disappearances that were never solved, 4,000 political killings and approximately 1,500 reported kidnappings.[39] Multiply that by the factor of unreported cases and you're looking at roughly 15,000 kidnappings that actually took place in one year alone in that country. Those numbers have dropped considerably over the past decade due to growing stability in Columbia and a reduction in tensions with the FARC.

---

[39] www.amnestyusa.org

After hurricane Jeanne in 2004, where Haiti lost a major portion of income-producing jobs, kidnappings for ransom skyrocketed. According to the US Embassy Consular, in 2006 there were over 600 "reported" kidnappings including 60 Americans working in the country. In 2008, after the country began to stabilize, those numbers dropped to 266 with only 27 Americans being taken hostage. Then in 2009, the numbers dropped to just 73; however, after the 2010 devastation from the earthquake, the number of American kidnappings soon rose to approximately one every three days due to lack of any available employment in the region.[40] As the country has rebuilt, those numbers are starting to drop. While conducting your pre-travel research, kidnapping numbers, trends and hot spots need to be investigated.

Many Americans are under the false belief that good old Uncle Sam will come charging in to their rescue should they be kidnapped in a foreign country. Unfortunately, that just doesn't happen. There is the rare exception with military, political personnel or a few highly publicized people who may be rescued by US Special Forces. These events are few and far between.

The official US policy on hostages and hijackings states: "When Americans are abducted overseas the US government looks to the *host government* to exercise its responsibility under international law to protect all persons within its territory and bring about the safe release of the hostages."[41]

So if you are traveling to Haiti, Ghana, Ethiopia, or any of a long list of underdeveloped countries, take a look at the

---

[40] www.osac.gov
[41] www.fam.state.gov

local law enforcement and just imagine for a moment how well they are prepared to come to your rescue should the need arise. That's not saying anything bad about the law enforcement in these countries, just that they simply don't have the manpower, funding or training like we do here in the US.

There are a number of specific things that you can do to prevent yourself from becoming the victim of a kidnapping, not that you can prevent everything, but with proper training you can actually prevent the vast majority of these incidents. That is why this book was written. I hope to provide you with some basic knowledge, skills and practices that may help you stay out of harm's way.

First, a good portion of the knowledge that has been included up to this point will go a long way in opening your eyes to the kidnappers' actions associated with choosing and taking a hostage, situational awareness being the most important. But there are a few other things that are very specific to kidnappings that you should also be aware of and pay attention to during your travels to countries that have a known issue with kidnappings.

With the rare exception, kidnappings take place at a chokepoint, either near the victim's residence/hotel or where they work. Between these two points the victim can travel by a number of different routes or divert to different locations for a number of different reasons, but the common factor is that they always end up at either the place where they work or the place where they sleep, i.e. a chokepoint.

The second criteria common to attack sites for kidnappings is that the victim becomes predictable. The victim can be found at one of these chokepoints at the exact same time and place each day. Think about your own life between Monday and Friday. You get up and leave for work at exactly 7:30 every morning and drive down the same side road before you reach the main highway. At 5:02 every day you leave your office and head home, usually arriving at 5:30, give or take a little, depending on your wife's need for you to run by the drug store or stop at the grocery and pick up a gallon of milk. Five days per week your movements will be very predictable and will almost always place you at one of these chokepoints at a specific time. If someone wanted to take you hostage, where would they go? Someplace near one of these chokepoints.

The next criterion for the attack site will be someplace where they are able to observe and pattern your movements. With rare exception, kidnapping victims have been watched for weeks by their attackers in order to gain a good pattern on their movements and plan the attack. Unless they are properly trained, most kidnappers can be detected during their pre-attack surveillance utilizing the same techniques I discussed in chapter 8 on Situational Awareness and being watched or followed.

The other criterion is the ability to escape once the kidnapping has taken place. These people want to be able to take you hostage and then get out of the area and to a location where they are in control as quickly as possible.

High profile businessmen and their security personnel take hard looks at these chokepoints and study these attack criteria. They consciously vary their departure times and routes of travel. They will look at each chokepoint to see which ones have the best opportunity for escape and then concentrate their attention on identifying the pre-kidnapping surveillance teams in these areas. These are known as surveillance detection zones, and even you, as an individual traveler, should pay attention to who is watching you at these locations.

Statistics from security firms have shown that approximately 80% of these attacks can be prevented when proper techniques are employed. Unfortunately, about 90% are successful. This is because, coming from their own words after their recovery, most people simply denied the possibility that they could ever be a victim of a kidnapping. That possibility was waved off as "it will never happen to me!" but it does happen, even to the most seasoned travelers. Americans need to realize and understand their value to a kidnapping organization.

So, once you identify the chokepoints, what should you look for? We discussed many of these items in chapters 7, 8 and 10. You are looking for the mistakes, things that are simply not normal. I've rarely been in a foreign country, either by myself or with just one or two other travelers, for more than 3 or 4 days where I was not being watched or followed. These people usually become quite obvious at the chokepoints by the way they observe you. If you are able to watch using your peripheral vision without actually looking directly at a person who is watching you, you'll see their faces track your every movement as you pass by their position. Once you've seen it, it will actually become very obvious from that day forward. Most kidnappers are not trained in proper surveillance techniques and their actions will almost always give them away to a person who pays attention to their surroundings and knows what to look for.

The first thing you need to do is pay attention to everyone sitting or standing around or anywhere near your chokepoints each and every time you come or go. Do you see the same people repeatedly? Once you start to observe and recognize these people, have you ever seen any of them at both locations: where you work and where you live? If you have, unless they are working with you on a project, there is a 99.9% certainty that you are being followed and targeted for something. Of those people you see repeatedly at either location, do any of them watch and follow your movements? Do they get on the phone as soon as you arrive or pass by? These are all clues to the fact that someone is monitoring your movements.

One proactive security option is to let these people know that you are aware that they are watching you. On occasion I will stop and look directly at this person and, just like I discussed in the subway scenario, make it very obvious that I am remembering what they look like from head to toe. Sometimes I'll even give them a smile and a wave followed by this memorization drill. I've actually seen these people quickly get up and leave when they knew that they too were being closely observed. When this happened, was there any doubt that they were following me? Absolutely none! My actions very well may have prevented me from becoming a victim.

I remember one specific time in Mexico City when I was followed every time I left my hotel for two days straight by a Mexican male in his 20s. I was there on business and couldn't leave so I decided to let him know that I'd had enough. As I left the hotel and walked down the street to go have dinner, I was able to use the reflection in the windows across the street to confirm that my observer was following as usual. As I reached an intersection that permitted me to continue observing his approach in the windows across the street, I made the turn, took four steps around the corner, stopped, turned around and waited for him to follow. As he came around the corner we met face to face, at which time I asked him, "What's up?" (Que Pasa?) The expression of shock and panic on his face said more than I can put into words. This was followed by two things, one I expected and the other I did not!

First, this young man turned around and took off running as fast as he could go. This I expected. What I did not expect was to see another young Mexican male observe the incident and take off running after his partner. I had never noticed the second man who was following me. The good part of this encounter is that, to my knowledge, I was not followed again during my two-week stay in Mexico City. I'm guessing they decided to choose a less intimidating victim!

Many church groups and mission teams have asked me about how to dress when working in a foreign country. Normally I tell everyone to try to blend into the local environment as much as possible; however, if you are travelling or working in a large group, sometimes it may be better to stand out than to blend in.

You've heard it said, "There's safety in numbers." I believe that. Criminals want to choose a single, passive individual or maybe a couple of people at most. They don't want to go up against an entire group of people no matter how docile they may be. My advice to large traveling parties is to consider buying group shirts or jackets that all look alike and make them fairly bright. Do not include American symbols like our flag or the name of a world renowned town like New York City. Using a symbol from the local country may be seen as a sign of respect. A group of 15 to 20 people, all dressed alike and traveling together will rarely be the target of criminal activity. It's only when individuals wander off by themselves that they run into trouble.

So, what do you do when it becomes very obvious that you are being watched, followed or targeted? The first thing to do is admit the fact that you have an issue and the second is to make everyone in your traveling party aware of it. Then collectively you need to decide what to do. Maybe it would be a good idea to tell the local authorities about the situation and see if they will confront these people. Maybe you should make a major change, like moving to another hotel? At the absolute least, you and your group need to change your patterns, leave at a different time each day, use a different entrance or exit to the hotel and travel by different routes to your destination. If you can break the predictable pattern, you'll put the advantage at least a little more in your court. Depending on the specifics of the situation, sometimes it may be best to simply pack up and go home when there is a specific, credible threat to your personal safety and security.

13

Basics of Hostage Survival

Having a basic understanding about what to expect, what to do or not do, when all of your safety and security precautions failed and you find yourself the victim of a kidnapping can pay huge dividends in surviving a hostage situation. Knowing the information covered in this chapter can greatly improve your odds of coming home safely to your loved ones.

What type of person goes out and takes another person hostage? Kidnappers usually fall into one of four basic categories with variations that may include parts and pieces from each of the following:

Political Extremists are people who believe what they are doing is justified in order to get their political issues resolved. In South America the FARC is a good example of this category. The FARC wants to overthrow the government and take control of the country under their version of Communist rule. For decades the FARC has been one of the most prolific kidnapping organizations in the world taking hostages that include politicians, soldiers or police officers.

Criminal kidnappings are those which are conducted specifically for financial gain. The FARC also falls into this category as they are well known for taking just about anyone hostage who will bring them a good ransom which can be used to purchase weapons and supplies. Many Americans have been taken hostage by the FARC including government personnel, businessmen and women, and many missionaries like jungle pilot Russell Stendal who wrote the book *Rescue the Captors* to chronicle his ordeal.

Criminal kidnappings have become a full time business around the world. Kidnappings for financial gain take place almost daily by countless criminal organizations along with terrorist factions such as al-Qaeda in Iraq, Pakistan and Afghanistan, the Philippines and Yemen. Many hostages are taken for financial gain right here in America too! It was widely reported in 2009 and 2010 that Phoenix, Arizona had the second highest kidnapping rate in the world, falling just behind Mexico City in the statistics.[42]

The kidnapping of young girls by criminal organizations is a Billion-dollar industry. These girls are taken and then quickly smuggled out of their home country and sold into the sex trade industry around the world. The sad truth is that many of the missing women here in America, those who are never located, were actually kidnapped and smuggled into countries like China, Turkey and other foreign locations where young American women are considered exotics.

Religious Fanatics are another category that takes thousands of hostages each year. Al-Qaeda would fall into this category when they, as a Muslim terrorist organization, specifically take Christians hostage because of their faith. You also see this take place in locations like the Philippines, China and many of the African nations.

Terrorist kidnappings, although not listed as a specific category, generally fall into one of the three categories listed above depending on the specifics of the case.

Mentally Disturbed people comprise the final category. You'll find these people in every country, in any culture,

---

[42] http://www.politifact.com/texas/statements/2010/jun/28/john-mccain/mccain-says-phoenix-second-kidnapping-capital-worl/

and their motivation does not revolve around politics, financial gain or religious freedoms. The kidnapping of Jaycee Dugard in 1991 and Elizabeth Smart in 2002 are prime examples where mentally deranged individuals took young girls hostage for their own personal reasons.

Using the knowledge gained in this book will certainly help open your eyes to the dangers that kidnappers present; however, modern, professional kidnapping organizations have learned tactics to hide the identity of their operatives so that they may not appear to be who they actually are. One prime example that these organizations have learned to use over the years is the utilization of beautiful young women to lure their victims into a location more advantageous to the kidnappers.

These girls and young women are not perceived as a possible threat by most travelers. As an example, consider the 20-something young ladies who meet American men in the nightclubs to party and dance the night away. These ladies are not seen by their victims as being a threat, at least not until after they've left the club and have lured their victims into their apartment where their partners in crime are ready and waiting.

Another example might be the innocent looking 6-year-old girl who runs up to the American couple in the local market, crying her eyes out, telling them that her poor grandmother has fallen, needs help and begs for their assistance. With the American culture being caring and always willing to lend a hand, this couple follows the young girl through the market, down the alley and around the corner where their lives will change forever.

Of course, it only makes sense to avoid the first scenario, but think about the situation with the young, crying girl in the market for a moment. When you stop and seriously consider the situation logically, this girl probably grew up in that market and knows everyone there by their first names. Why would she be coming up to complete strangers from a foreign country, begging for assistance with her injured grandmother? She wouldn't! I'm not saying that you shouldn't go help her, what I am saying is that before you rush in to help, you need to take just a moment to stop and think about the situation logically. Tell this girl to hold on for a moment while you go find a police officer who can go with her and provide assistance. If she is still there when you find the police officer, then go and assist; however, if, when you say you're going to get the police, you turn around and she's suddenly disappeared into the crowd, stop and say your prayers! This moment of clarity may very well have just saved your life!

Now that I've discussed the general categories of the kidnappers, are there any general categories for the hostages? Hostages are normally taken for a number of different reasons. Depending on where you'll be traveling, understanding why you would be considered a viable target will help open your eyes to taking preventative precautions.

When it comes to a kidnapping for ransom, the number one criteria for selecting victims is that they are valuable to someone. Your organization, church or family members will do whatever it takes to get you home and this is what the kidnappers are looking for. Simply the fact that you are an American means that you are valuable to someone. Americans, even the poorest college students, probably have more money in their checking accounts than most people in the world make in a month or even a year. All

Americans are perceived as wealthy and by most standards we are. If you are on a mission trip, working with a big organization or large church, then you are probably at the top of the list when it comes to being selected as a possible victim.

Political kidnappings generally target prominent people such as a mayor, police chief or military personnel but, depending on what you are doing in the country, you very well may fall into this category too.

The next two categories are:

- People hated by their captors and,
- People seen as a source of trouble.

If you are on a church mission trip and traveling into a non-Christian country, you fully meet the criteria for both of these categories. Even American businessmen and women can fit into this category. Americans may be unwanted in the country by many people and, depending on why you are in their country your mission team may be perceived as a source of trouble to a terrorist organization.

The last category is people who are just in the wrong place at the wrong time. These people are simply victims of circumstance. You may be the nicest person in the world, traveling overseas on nothing more than a personal vacation, when you accidentally wander into the wrong place at the wrong time.

For the purposes of this book and teaching, let's say you find yourself in a kidnapping situation and it's no longer a matter of how to stay out of trouble but a matter of how to survive the situation in order to make it home to your friends and family. Every person who has been the unfortunate victim of a hostage situation goes through four very distinctive psychological phases during his or her captivity. It's only a matter of the individual's ability to handle major stress events along with any prior training that will determine how long each person lingers in each of these different phases. They are: *Shock, Reality, Adaptation* and *Traumatic Depression.*

The first phase that every hostage goes through during the initial phase of a kidnapping is shock and disbelief. "This isn't really happening" or, "Although this looks bad, everything is going to be Okay." are the most common thoughts for every hostage as the kidnapping commences. Nobody wants to believe that he or she is about to be the victim of a kidnapping and what those consequences mean in terms of his or her life. It's an overwhelming fear that nobody is prepared to accept.

How long you stay in this phase all depends on the situation and on your personal internal make-up. Some people choose denial for hours or even days, not willing to mentally accept the truth of their situation. They subconsciously use denial as a coping mechanism so that they don't have to consciously accept their fate; however, at some point the reality of the situation sets in which leads us to the next phase: Reality.

When the victim's mental state suddenly accepts the fact that he or she has been taken hostage and this situation isn't going to simply go away on its own, the change happens as rapidly as someone flipping on a light switch. They are suddenly overcome and overwhelmed with a feeling of total despair. Many hostages have described the change as though it were a physical weight being placed upon the victim's shoulders.

In 2001, while working an operation in South America, I too, even with all of my training and experience, became the victim of a kidnapping, so I speak from first-hand experience. At first I thought that surly this issue would resolve itself and we'd be heading back to our hotel within just a few minutes. Then, after what seemed like an eternity but was probably more like just a minute or two, the reality of the situation set in. We (there were three of us) were going to be taken hostage.

For years I used to tell people that:

- When the reality of the situation set in, it happened so suddenly that it was just as quick as when someone walks into the room and flips on the lights.

- When the reality of the situation set in, it literally felt as though someone had just placed a two-inch-thick concrete bathrobe onto my shoulders.

I used to think this description was a little strange until I read a book by former hostage, Gracia Burnham.

Gracia and her husband Martin were working in the Philippines when they were taken hostage.[43] Their kidnapping actually had nothing to do with their jobs. The Burnham's were taking a break from their work in the field and celebrating their anniversary by staying at a vacation resort when a division of the Abu Sayyef took over the resort one night. These men were looking for rich victims staying at the resort in a kidnapping for ransom operation.

---

[43] In the Presence of my Enemies by Gracia Burnham

In her book, *In the Presence of My Enemies*, Gracia describes her ordeal and how she handled being a Christian woman held by Islamic men. Gracia describes the moment that the reality phase of her kidnapping set in with the following statement, "I turned to Martin with a heaviness starting to 'push down upon my shoulders.' "We are in BIG trouble," she said.

Gracia, along with many other hostages I've talked to over the years, described the physical feeling of an actual weight pressing down on their shoulders at the exact moment the reality of the situation set in. It's a phenomenon that is common to the vast majority of hostages when the reality of the situation sets in.

They say that in life-threatening situations your life flashes before your eyes. In my case, as in most others, that is exactly what happens. Due to the overload of emotions, your brain will begin to flash an amazing array of thoughts from times past through your memory banks in order to cope with the situation. This is an automatic defensive response by your brain when it's trying to protect itself. You are aware of what is happening and you'll remember it later but at the time your brain is using this memory flash as a way to protect you from accepting the reality of the situation.

So how long do people stay in this reality phase of the kidnapping? Best answer, it all depends on the individual and any training on this issue they may have received. I do know that the quicker you can get out of this shut-down, total despair, mental protective phase, the quicker you can get into the adaptation phase and start concentrating on surviving the ordeal.

In my case, the one thought that flashed through my mind, a thought that was totally overwhelming, which snapped me out of the reality phase and on to the next was the most despairing thought I've ever had in my life. You see, in our situation, we were not being taken hostage for any financial gain. We were federal law enforcement agents working a case against a major South American cartel and there was only one outcome to our situation, and it wasn't a good one. The saddest thought that I've ever had in my life was that my wife and children would never have any closure regarding their husband and father who went missing during a business trip to South America. No one would ever find our bodies. We were working on our own without support in an undercover capacity, so no one would know what really happened; therefore, our families would never have closure or an explanation and would never have a body to bury. We were simply going to disappear.

It was at this point that my mind suddenly flashed back to a power point slide that I saw during a survival training class taught by Emergency Response International that I attended about three years prior. That slide looked like this:

Surviving the Hostage Situation
The 4 Psychological Phases:
- Shock
- Reality
- Adaptation
- Traumatic Depression

At the exact moment of that thought I suddenly remembered this slide along with the advice we had been given about what to do next. Just like a light switch, I snapped out of the reality phase and into the adaptation phase and immediately started concentrating on survival. I leaned over to my partner, made a simple comment to him and he had the exact same reaction. My partner later told me that he had been experiencing these exact same thoughts and feelings, at virtually the exact same time, and as soon as I said something to him he snapped out of the reality phase and into the adaptation phase in an instant, too.

So, now that you've gotten mentally moved into the adaptation phase what do you do? Well, it all depends on your situation, but the main thing you must do is to look at what is taking place and learn to adapt to the situation in order to survive this ordeal and make it home once it's over. It's this adaptation phase that you need to get to and stay in, in order to survive the hostage situation!

In the previous chapter I talked about criteria common to all kidnapping attack sites. One of these criteria was the ability to escape and move you to a place where they have control. That's the first thing that will happen if you are ever taken hostage in a kidnapping situation. Your kidnappers will move you as quickly as possible from a location where they are not in full control to a location where they are. In most cases this relocation will come in the form of a vehicle and they will move you as quickly as possible into one of their safe houses.

It's in this first 15 to 45 minutes of relocation, when nothing is fully in their control that may open the opportunity for you to escape. This information was on the second power point slide that flashed across my mind during our kidnapping situation and was included in the words from me that snapped my partner out of his reality phase, "We need to get out of this and I have a plan."

Of course this is also the time when the armed kidnappers are at their most insecure place and much more willing to shoot and kill their victims than any other time during the kidnapping operation. So you as the victim need to decide the best course of action to take. That's why it is so important to move from the reality phase to the adaptation phase as quickly as you can. It allows you to start making good rational decisions about your situation and survival.

Should you attempt to escape or not? It's a question that every hostage will ask himself at some point during his ordeal. Of course the more control the kidnappers have over their victims, the least likely an escape will be possible. It's in the first part of the kidnapping, before they get you secured into their safe house that affords the best possibility for a successful escape.

Before making the decision to escape, the first question you should ask yourself is, "Why have I been taken hostage?"

This is where the information about the different types of kidnappings and the research you did on the country before leaving home becomes critically important. Is this a criminal act with the objective of getting a ransom paid for financial gain? The fact that more than 80% of kidnappings for ransom end with the successful return of the hostage tells you that if this is a kidnapping for ransom, you may want to simply stay where you are and keep yourself alive until it's over. In this case you would have an 8 in 10 chance of going home. Those aren't bad odds.

On the other hand, if this kidnapping is a terrorist act (political or religious), then there is very little chance that you will make it home. So, if you get killed during an escape attempt, what have you lost? Nothing!

So what would constitute this decision for an escape attempt? Take a look at my situation. We were not being taken hostage for any financial gain. At best, it could be considered a political kidnapping but it was probably more like a murder in progress than anything else.

What about the case where a Christian missionary is working in a Muslim country and taken hostage by Islamic terrorists? The objective or motive of the kidnappers would not be for any financial gain, it would be to rid their country of this hated source of trouble. The final outcome would probably not be the safe release of the victim.

If you decide that an escape is the only option or at least your best option, it's the first 15 to 45 minutes that will usually provide the best opportunity for a successful escape. You'll have to weigh all of the factors, make the proper decision and get your mind working well enough that you can concentrate on looking for a possible escape route.

One word of good advice: If you decide that you are going to attempt to escape from the kidnappers, forget the word "attempt." If you are not successful in making your escape, the final outcome is not something you want to be thinking about. (The chances are that if you don't make it, you probably won't survive the day.)

The second good piece of advice is: Don't let them know what you are thinking and when you act, act quickly and decisively. It needs to be unexpected and committed with 100% of all the strength, power and stamina you have in your mind and body! Other than this advice, everything else would be contingent on your particular circumstances.

So, for a training scenario, let's say you've been kidnapped and you have determined that the reason for being taken hostage is for ransom which most kidnappings are. Unless a really good opportunity arises for a successful escape, it's probably better to adapt to the situation, concentrate on surviving and settle in for the long haul. This situation won't resolve itself overnight.

One of the first things a victim can do to help adapt to the situation starts as you are being taken away from the attack site. Try to concentrate on memorizing the route taken from where you were, to where you will be held. When your ransom is paid, don't expect your kidnappers to simply drive up to your hotel, business, or the police station and let you out where they could be captured. More than likely they will drop you off somewhere just outside of a main town and there is a good chance that it will be along the road they used to escape from that town after the attack.

Try to visualize the route and remember as many details as possible. Even if you are unable to see outside, take note of the turns you made, the street noises that may be unique to the road such as the noise from a factory, the smell and sounds of the local market. Try to track the time it takes to travel between towns or between turns off the main road. All of these things may not only help you get home once released, but will give your mind something to start doing in order to keep it from concentrating on the psychological overload of being kidnapped so you can focus on surviving the ordeal.

"I was steeling myself to stay calm, trying to stay focused as each event unfolded," states Gracia Burnham in her book. "I was also working to recall a class I had taken back in the late 1980s, to prepare the teams for hostage situations."

When you talk to anyone who has been held as a hostage, who ever attended any type of even basic hostage survival training, you find that this information was a huge advantage in helping them survive the event. Knowing what to expect, what to do, what to watch out for and what to avoid can be a lifesaver when it comes to the final outcome. Many hostages (that other 20% who don't come home) often do things during their captivity that cause their own demise. It's in this basic training and the purpose for writing this chapter that provides people with the knowledge of these issues so they can either be avoided or properly dealt with.

There are a few things that happen to virtually every hostage that, when these issues are anticipated, make them more likely to survive. In fact, it's when these things happened but were not anticipated that demoralized the victims and was the catalyst that sent many into the last phase, traumatic depression that we'll talk about shortly.

Virtually every hostage can expect to be stripped right down to their birthday suits and thoroughly searched. This is usually nothing personal against the victim. The kidnappers want to make sure you are not hiding anything. They will usually want to get you out of your American clothing and exchange it for something the locals would be wearing. This is because if you were accidentally seen by any of the local populous, it would bring immediate attention to you and them.

You can also anticipate and expect to be tied up and locked up for long periods of time. Most Americans, when they think about being taken hostage, think about being locked in a small dark room somewhere and often that is exactly what happens, but in many cases the victim is also tied up or even chained to something like a tree in the middle of the forest. This is especially true for those who may have tried to escape and failed or those who are abstinent or cause trouble.

Deciding to survive the kidnapping ordeal until the ransom is paid is not the time to try to become a hero. It's the time to settle down and try to be the model prisoner! Calm yourself mentally, cooperate as much as possible and concentrate on surviving the ordeal. There's not a whole lot else you can do other than keeping yourself alive.

Hostages basically have one and only one job they must accomplish every day and that is to do everything they can to "*survive until they are released!*" Everything else is secondary. If you don't survive the ordeal, when the time comes to release you, it's a moot point.

Some of the things you need to do when it comes to surviving the ordeal are to keep both your mind and your body as active as possible. Many people simply shut down both and a number of hostages have simply dwindled down in mental and physical stamina to where they became sick and died. Anything you can do to stay organized and any exercise you can do, both with your mind and your body, will pay huge dividends in surviving the ordeal. Most hostages use prayer and meditation as a way to pass the time. Stagnant time is one of the hardest issues hostages must deal with.

Many hostages will mentally plan elaborate escapes and often communicate with other hostages to gain and share ideas on a successful escape even when none will ever be attempted. It's this mental planning thought process that keeps their minds active; it's a type of mental exercise.

You can expect to be relocated and moved quite often. This is done for a number of reasons; one, to keep law enforcement's ability to locate where they are holding you thrown off track. The other is to change the victim's guards for new ones as often as possible. Victims will often start to build a rapport with their captors, which can make things difficult when the ransom is not paid and they must make the decision on what to do with the hostage.

When you are relocated you should expect and anticipate the conditions at the new location to be nothing like the place you just left. Being moved from a location that had a bed (a mat on the floor) and a blanket to an empty floor, or even worse, being held outside tied like a dog to nothing more than a tree in the woods can completely demoralize many hostages. However, if the hostages expected to encounter these conditions each time they were relocated as a normal part of the process, the situation would only pose new obstacles and challenges for them to overcome.

As soon as you are settled into the location, start the process of memorizing everything in your new environment. Memorize where everything is located and especially the location of the safest place to hide should a rescue operation commence.

Hostages unable to speak the local language and therefore not able to communicate with their captors usually had a very difficult time keeping track of the correct date. Early in captivity hostages should devise a way to keep track of the date, day and time, and set up a daily schedule for themselves.

Often it was the issue of not being able to determine when some significant date had taken place that threw hostages into major traumatic depression. Had Christmas come and gone? Had we passed my birthday, anniversary or my child's birthday? Many hostages lost all track of what day it was, even what month it was after very short periods of time when they had not found a way to track the date. From the onset it would be a good mental practice to establish the date and then do your best to keep track of it.

When it comes to dealing with your captors one on one, it's best to treat them with as much respect as you are capable of doing. Remember that they are in control of everything in your life, so demonstrate an apparent sincerity when they talk to you.

One thing you should never do is to be rude or aggressive toward your captors. This is a lot easier said than done, especially when situations change for the worse. It's a natural tendency when a person is under extreme stress to lash out at the person who is causing that stress. In a hostage situation these actions need to be curtailed. Hostages who become uncooperative or even hostile towards their captors are statistically held much longer than those who cooperate. They are also subjected to considerably worse living conditions than those who try to be the model prisoner.

Repeatedly, many hostages reached the point where they would do nothing towards cooperating with their captors including having their picture taken. Ingrid Betancourt was held hostage by the FARC in Columbia for six years and went through many periods where she absolutely refused to cooperate in any way with her captors. She often refused to allow them to take pictures or videos of her; however, it was these pictures and videos which in the end helped intelligence personnel determine exactly what part of the country she was being held in and by whom, which ultimately resulted in her rescue.[44] So, allow photographs. In fact, encourage as many photo opportunities as you can. They could greatly help your situation.

Your best option in dealing with your captors is to cooperate as best you can with every situation as it unfolds and, as much as possible, do not portray fear to your captors. Many captors want to see you cower or beg in order to demonstrate dominance over your condition. Try instead to humanize yourself and, when possible, build a little rapport with them. If you are able to do nothing other than get your captors to understand that you are freezing at night, to the point that they provide you with a blanket, you've made significant progress in getting them to see you as a human being and not just an animal chained to a tree.

Now, for women this can be a very fine line to walk, especially for single women. Gracia Burnham wrote about the consequences of being a captive woman extensively in her book. She talked about a number of other women who were taken hostage along with her in the Philippines. Some were single when the ordeal began and others, regardless of marital status, were forced to declare that they were single during their year of captivity in order to be taken as wives by their Muslim captors.

Tom Howes was held off and on with Ingrid Betancourt by the FARC. In his book, *Out of Captivity*, he had this to say

---

[44] Out of Captivity by Marc Gonsalves, Keith Stansell and Tom Howes

about his captors: "Do not expect your captors to operate by anything resembling the logic or values that we do!"

Being held for over five years, Tom came to realize that from birth these people were raised in a culture so different from ours that their actions defied any logic that we as Americans could understand. They truly did not process common thoughts the way we do. Understanding this cultural concept helped him to cope with the situation when nothing around him made any sense at all.

Before I move on to traumatic depression, I'd like to discuss a psychological anomaly that many of you have probably heard of but never truly understood. Stockholm Syndrome is a psychological adaptation that happens when hostages are repeatedly threatened with death by their captors and then allowed to live. After this scenario happens repeatedly, the victims come to believe that they owe their lives to the captors for not being killed.

The name came from a botched bank robbery that happened in Stockholm, Sweden.[45] During the robbery all of the employees and patrons of the bank were taken hostage. Many were paraded out in front of the police and told that they would be executed if the demands were not met. Some hostages were actually killed, but others were spared at the last moment, being told that they were being allowed to live only because the bank robbers had mercy on them.

When the event was over, many of the hostages refused to testify against their captors feeling that they owed them a debt of gratitude for not being killed during the ordeal. Some of the female hostages even developed romantic

---

[45] www.medical-dictionary.thefreedictionary.com/Stockholm+syndrome

relationships with their captors during their prison sentences. The name of the town where all this took place has now been made synonymous with the syndrome.

Traumatic Depression is the last of the four psychological phases that we will discuss, and every hostage held for any length of time will struggle with traumatic depression during their captivity. Traumatic depression happens when the hostages reach the point where they simply give up on their plight and want to die.

Many have been heard saying, "I'd rather die than spend another day living like this," and many actually do. Psychologically they have had enough and mentally check out to the point that many stop eating and drinking. They get run down physically to the point where they get sick and their bodies make no attempt to fight off the disease, so they die.

Traumatic depression often takes hold when one of the situations we spoke about earlier in this chapter takes place, like being moved to a holding area that is much worse than the conditions they had before. Can you imagine going from being held in a room with a bed to being chained to a tree in the pouring rain, being beaten, sexually assaulted (both men and women can suffer this issue), becoming sick with dysentery, or it may simply be from the despair of being held past your breaking point.

The first step in handling traumatic depression is to understand that it is something that will happen if you are held long enough and anticipate that you'll have to deal with it at some point. The second step is to recognize the depression when it does happen and do something to avoid it or find a way to get out of the depression as soon as it starts. The first time you say to yourself that you'd rather die than spend another day in captivity, stop, realize what is happening and do something constructive to get back to concentrating on keeping yourself alive!

Marc Gonsalves, Tom Howes and Keith Stansell, while working a government contract in the southern part of Columbia, were held for over five years by the FARC after the aircraft they were operating suffered a catastrophic engine failure. In their book, *Out of Captivity*, Marc describes how he handled his battles with traumatic depression. Marc suffered repeated bouts of dysentery which really depleted his body. He understood the effects of traumatic depression and when he was struggling, Marc began to make small chess sets out of grass, soap and pieces of wood.

Marc had been a competitive chess player before he was taken hostage, and building chess sets took weeks and sometimes months to complete. During the time he spent making chess pieces, and while he was playing chess with other hostages (at times he even played chess with his captors. Can you say building rapport?), Marc said that he no longer felt like a hostage. He concentrated so hard on his tasks of making the pieces or playing the game that his mind simply blanked out everything that was happening around him.

Recognizing and avoiding traumatic depression can change the outcome for a hostage, to coming home rather than dying during captivity. You need to prepare for the unexpected! When your mental state begins to slip and you have those first thoughts that you'd rather just give up and die than spend another day in captivity, it's time to realize what is happening, find some way to rebuild and maintain that positive mental attitude to keep yourself alive.

One option that many hostages have used to combat the effects of traumatic depression was to plan for an escape. This helped even when an escape wasn't even remotely possible. The simple act of mentally planning an escape gave the hostages something to do. Many spent hours, even days, looking at every aspect of their detention and surroundings to find any possible opportunity.

Many hostages communicated with other captives to gain ideas on what they might have observed and worked together on elaborate escape plans. They also fabricated small escape kits such as a needle and thread to use as fishing gear or to sew up a wound, a few coins, tape or a flashlight. It didn't matter that they would never use them, it was simply the fact that they were able to concentrate on something positive and proactive that kept their minds from thinking about how bad their life had become and kept them from sinking into depression. Regardless of what you do, you must admit the possibility of traumatic depression, plan for it and find a way to avoid it.

14

Resolution

The victim has done his or her job by doing everything necessary in order to survive the hostage situation. Unknown to the hostage, the time has come where he or she is either going to be released or is going to be rescued. There are three basic ways this is going to take place.

One, the demands of the kidnappers have been met (the ransom was paid or the prisoners were released, etc.), and the kidnappers in turn are going to set you free. With rare exceptions, they are not going to just drive up to the front door of your hotel or the local police station and let you out. More than likely they will blindfold you and transport you to a location where you will be let out and can make your way to someplace nearby for assistance.

Two, the demands were not met but you've been able to build enough rapport with your captors that instead of eliminating you as a witness (you are now able to identify many of these people and possibly where you were being held), and they decide to simply release you out of the kindness of their hearts. This will probably happen in the same manner as described in option one.

Third, there is a dramatic rescue by law enforcement or military personnel: the Calvary comes charging in with guns blazing, and they sweep you away to safety.

For the first two resolution options there isn't a whole lot you can do to improve your chances for a safe return other than those discussed in the previous chapter; however, there are a number of things that hostages can do or have done during dramatic rescues that have either greatly improved their odds of surviving the ordeal or, if done wrong, have caused hostages to be seriously injured or killed. In this chapter I will discuss specifics on what these issues are and what you, as a hostage, should or should not do during a rescue attempt.

Long before any rescue ever takes place, hostages should anticipate a dramatic rescue happening at any time and keep this anticipation going to the end of the ordeal. Many hostages, who were rescued after fairly significant lengths of time, told their rescuers that they were completely caught off guard because they had given up long ago on any hopes of a rescue. Hostages need to not only anticipate a rescue but also plan ahead for it.

One of the first things a hostage should do when he or she is moved to a new location is to identify the safest place to go during a rescue operation from a security standpoint. As an example, if you were being held inside a building that included a bathroom, the safest place to go would be on the floor between the toilet and tub or sink. Just like during a tornado, this area provides the greatest amount of protection from outside dangers like flying debris, or in a rescue attempt, bullets coming through walls.

But what if you were being held in a jungle in the middle of nowhere? Your safe location may be behind a table, a tree, a log on the ground or some other structure that provides protection. If nothing else, at least try to find a low spot in the terrain that will provide some level of protection. After the gunshots begin flying is not the time to try and figure out where you need to go!

Your safe spot should be planned well in advance. In fact, it should be one of the first tasks you accomplish after being moved to a new location so that you will go there instinctively at the first sounds of trouble.

If you are being held in a location where there is no place to hide (as an example, you are being held in a square room with no protection at all), the best thing to do would be to lay face down in the middle of the room with your hands clasped behind your head or straight out to your side. Think about the police videos you've watched on TV. The policeman will place the suspect face down on the ground with his hands behind his head in a safe, non-threatening position.

Why should you assume this position? After even a few days in captivity, especially if your captors have changed your clothes, you may not be immediately recognizable to your rescuers as the hostage. To a soldier or police officer coming into the building on a rescue operation, seeing someone in this position (hostage or kidnapper) indicates to the officer that this person is not going to cause him any trouble. Once your rescuers have made the area safe, they will be calling your name trying to locate the hostage.

So, after weeks or even months in captivity you suddenly hear yelling or maybe a few gunshots, the first thing you need to do, *without hesitation*, is to move as quickly as possible to your safe location, lie face down if possible and place your hands on top of your head. The next thing is to listen carefully to what is being said and if you are given specific orders, do *exactly* what you are told. If they tell you to get down, hit the deck! If they say to run, go as fast as you can and don't stop until you are told to!

Now for the things you should not do! I learned this first-hand many years ago when I worked on the rescue team for a couple of hostage recoveries in the Caribbean. We were briefed all of the issues in detail. These were things that have gotten hostages killed repeatedly over the years by their rescuers during rescue attempts.

One thing that can get a hostage killed by his rescuers often happens in a scenario like this: The kidnapper guarding the hostage is shot, drops his weapon and the hostage, thinking he is assisting in his rescue, picks up the weapon.

Think about this from a police officer's perspective for a moment. You run into a building where you know bad people with weapons are holding the hostage and they are probably willing to do anything in order to escape. You break into a room with your adrenaline running at full speed and see someone holding a weapon. What would your initial reaction be? Anyone holding a weapon is very likely to get shot by the police.

Rule number one: *NEVER PICK UP A WEAPON.* Additionally, stay as far away from weapons as possible!

The second thing that has gotten a hostage killed was that he ran outside the building toward his rescuers. Again, this goes back to how a hostage looks after just a few days in captivity. Many times even his own family members won't recognize him at first, so you can only imagine what a police officer, who's never met the hostage will think when they see some mad person, dressed in local clothing running toward them with his arms out. Many hostages have been accidently shot by the rescue teams thinking they were either being assaulted or that one of the kidnappers was trying to escape.

Rule number two: *NEVER RUN TO YOUR RESCUERS.* It's best to just be patient, go to your safe location, stay as far away from weapons and your former captors as possible and wait for the rescuers to come to you.

15

Legal Consideration

For those of you who are pastors, travel team leaders or in a safety or security management position within your church or organization, you do need to be concerned about the likelihood of litigation if something were to go wrong during one of your churches mission trips. In today's era of litigation, people sue over some of the smallest of issues. Quite often, during a major loss, it may be the spouse, parents or siblings of someone who was either killed or seriously injured who will bring the lawsuit against the church or sending organization.

Why the church? That's very simple; it's the number of dollars available. Attorneys will go to where the money is and most churches that send mission teams on international travel are generally well funded.

The jury's job in these cases is to look at the evidence being presented and then determine who is responsible for the loss. Once this is determined they must place a dollar figure to that loss when awarding damages. Their decision on who is responsible must be broken down into two basic categories: Was this loss caused by an Act of God or was it an Act of Omission. Let's take a look at a couple of examples to help explain the difference.

On January 12, 2010, during the earthquake in Port Au Prince, Haiti, Lynn University lost 6 people consisting of 4 students and 2 faculty members who were on a short-term educational trip, staying at the Hotel Montana which collapsed during the quake.[46] What could Lynn University

---

[46] www.lynn.edu/haiti

have done to protect their people from this tragedy? Nothing! This was an Act of God. The Hotel Montana was the finest hotel in the area. Nelson Mandela stayed there during his visit to Haiti and it was a common place for well-funded college travel teams to stay. Could Lynn University have done anything to prevent the earthquake? No, it was an Act of God so Lynn University had very little liability in the deaths of their faculty or the students, and therefore few if any damages would be awarded to the families for their losses.

Now let's jump back two years to this same location. There was a church that asked not to be named, that had a mission team staying at the same hotel, working at a location very near where the Lynn University students would have been. Their mission team arrived in Haiti and received the standard foreign country welcome briefing which lasted about 45 minutes and included a section on safety and security for the area. They were basically told to try and stay in groups when they traveled, avoid a couple of areas in town and try to avoid being out past dark.

A little after 5:00 p.m. three of the females on the trip departed the work site to walk back to the hotel (before dark, in a group). In route to the hotel they were grabbed by a small gang of young Haitian males who dragged them into an alley where they were sexually assaulted. One of the girls contracted HIV.

This church did not provide any specific dangers about the area, did not provide any of team members with the official travel warnings from the US Department of State, which had clear warnings about travel in the area, and did not conduct any specific safety or security training before departing on this trip.

The parents of this girl filed a negligence lawsuit against the church. The courts determined that the lack of this information and the short, insufficient in-country briefing on safety and security measures amounted to an Act of Omission. The financial awards to the family were such that the church had to empty its bank accounts and sell off all of its assets including the actual buildings in order to pay just a portion of the financial award judgment. This was an unfortunate situation for everyone involved.

So, hopefully, if you are a safety manager in the church, the mission's pastor or a travel team leader, you'll start to understand that there is a responsibility for you to properly prepare your mission teams before you send them out into the world. From a legal responsibility standpoint, the best you can do is to "Demonstrate" that you have provided:

- a. Safety
- b. Adequate Warnings
- c. Proper Preparation and Training

These are the three main criteria that the courts are going to look at when determining who was responsible for the loss.

So how do you "Demonstrate" this when/if something goes wrong? In a word, Documentation! You have to be able to lay a piece of paper on the table that shows you made a good faith effort to cover these areas of responsibility. Simply stating that you provided for these criteria is not going to hold a lot of weight in the courts system.

Safety – Providing safety will depend on the specific area of the world to which you are traveling. Did you provide safe transportation to get there and safe transportation while you were in the country? Did you use a taxi or private vehicle to transit a dangerous area or did you have your team members walk the short 10 minutes to the hotel? Did you provide safe accommodations, extra security when required or even recommended? There is no way to recommend all of the needed requirements for your specific trip as each will be uniquely different. Some places to which your mission teams travel will require more safety and security measures and some will require less.

Documenting your efforts to cover this area needs to be seriously considered by your trip team leader, mission's pastor or church safety manager. As an example, you can hand your mission teams a document that lets them know up front that they will be provided transportation to and from the work site and there will be a private security guard stationed at the entrance to the facility where they will be staying. That document can then be presented as evidence if the need arises.

Adequate Warnings – In the Appendix section of this book I provide a sample of an Emergency Action Plan. Emergency Action Plans must be completed and provided to every team member so that everyone knows what to do and where to go if anything goes wrong. My sample includes a section on current State Department Travel Warnings which must be completed for each location to be visited. For churches that don't have a staffed safety/security officer position that includes overseas travel issues, I recommend that pastors and team leaders meet with their team members a week or two prior to departure and have each team member independently research safety and security issues for the region they intend to visit, then rejoin at a later date to review all the different issues people find. You'll find that different people find different information which can be combined together and included as part of the emergency action plan.

Each team member should keep a copy of this plan with them at all times during their travels (it doesn't do any good if something happens when they are out and the emergency action plan is back at the hotel) and a copy should be kept at the churches main office. Having a documented emergency action plan that lists both the US State Department and local travel warnings along with where to go and what to do if something goes wrong not only helps your mission teams but it also provides good documentation should you ever need it for legal protection.

Proper Preparation and Training - In addition to gathering the information mentioned above, the mission teams should discuss the specific issues in the areas they intend to visit and what steps the team should employ to avoid these issues or what to do if they are encountered. If the trip involves extensive manual labor, a mandatory exercise program should be considered (and documented) to avoid medical issues. Education on the cultural and religious issues in the area should be discussed, especially when it involves security concerns and there can be a long list of other items included in this area, all of which should somehow be documented with the date that this training took place.

One very good option that many of the larger churches employ to cover these legal liability issues is to hire a professional company to come in and train their mission teams. Sometimes it's hard for churches to properly document their efforts in this area and often the courts don't feel that in-house training, regardless of how good it is, can adequately cover what is needed. The simple fact

241

that you hired a professional to train your mission teams takes that issue out of the picture and the company doing the training is able to testify on your behalf should it be required.[47]

Often pastors will ask the question, "What about the people who could not attend?" The fact is, you offered this training to the people who are traveling overseas and if they couldn't make it to the training for personal reasons, you've documented that you made the effort to provide proper preparation and training. If they missed the training for personal reasons, it places a good portion of the liability back on the individual traveler.

The other issue I commonly run up against is the cost. Of course, the cost of training is nothing compared to the attorney's fees on even the simplest of lawsuits, let alone any damage awards, but I understand that many churches are often working on a shoestring budget, especially for smaller churches and non-profit organizations.

I do have a suggestion for these small churches that decide to obtain professional training. Smaller churches may find it beneficial to pair up with several other local churches that conduct international travel to provide one training seminar for everyone. This has proven to have a number of benefits: people coming together and getting to know each other have often developed many new working relationships. In fact, I've seen churches that shared the cost of a seminar end up working together in cooperative efforts on many foreign projects. When the expense of the training is split between multiple churches, organizations or a small addition is added to the price of the mission trip, the cost to each is minimal.

---

[47] www.ihs-training.com

Regardless of any legal documentation concerns, the main purposes in covering these items are to protect your mission teams from harm and ensure that they have an enjoyable and successful trip!

16

Summary

I have covered a huge volume of safety and security information in the short context of this book, everything from how to pack your suitcase to surviving a hostage situation. That's a lot of information to cover all at one time but its good information that could someday very well save your life.

After reading all of the information in this book, I'd like to ask you, the reader, to answer this one simple question: "Will your next trip be safer now than it would have been before you read this book?"

The first answer you may jump to is: NO. Life suddenly seems a lot more dangerous now than it did before you read this book; however, if you'll stop for a moment and think about the reality of this question, you'll realize that the world is actually no different today than it was yesterday. Nothing has changed. The dangers that exist today, after you've read this book, have always existed; it's just that your eyes have been opened and you have been made aware of the dangers that have always existed. Walking through life from this day forward, your mind should automatically recognize the dangers, your intuition should kick in, allowing you to take action and avoid the dangers.

The correct answer to the question should be: YES. In fact, life is much safer for you after reading this book than it was before. You now know what to look for and should recognize the dangers without even thinking about them and you will be able to take proper action to avoid whatever issue you encounter.

This is what I call taking a proactive approach to your own personal safety and security. People who have been made aware of the dangers in life and taught how to recognize and avoid them are much safer and far less likely to be involved in an incident than those who walk blindly through life.

One of my favorite passages in the Bible regarding this approach to life comes from Matthew 10:16. "Behold, I send you forth as sheep in the midst of wolves: be ye therefore wise as serpents and harmless as doves." Many missionaries have used this passage in describing their daily lives in the mission's field.

John Gill completed an interesting exposition of the Bible with the following excerpt on Matthew 10:16.[48] It reads:

"The serpent is a very sharp sighted, cunning creature, and uses various arts and stratagems for its own preservation and especially of its head; and is so far to be imitated by the followers of Christ as to make use of all proper methods to preserve themselves from the insults and rage of men and not expose themselves to unnecessary dangers and to avoid all snares and traps that are laid for them."

John Gill truly understood the context of this verse! The interesting part of his excerpt is that it was written about American missionaries traveling to one of the wildest and most dangerous parts of the world, the American west back in the 1890s. Even though this passage was written over 100 years ago, it is just as applicable to your next mission trip as it was back then.

---

[48] www.biblestudytools.com/commentaries/gills-exposition-of-the-bible/matthew-10-16.html

This book covers an incredible amount of safety and security information, everything from what to pack to surviving a hostage situation. I sincerely pray that the information was helpful. What I see most often is that people who have attended my seminars are initially amazed at how many dangers they are suddenly aware of during the first few weeks after their eyes are opened. This is followed by a sense of calm and serenity as they come to realize that these dangers have always been there, always will be and that they are now able to walk through life recognizing and avoiding trouble before they walk into it.

Thank you for taking the time to read this book and when you're finished, please pass it along so others may benefit, not just people traveling on overseas mission trips but everyone you care for. Mothers, brothers, sisters, friends and neighbors, coworkers and the pastor at your church can all benefit.

In HIS service,
Brian

SEMINARS

IHS Trainings' primary business is providing current state-of-the-art seminars and training courses that educate people and provide them with the tools they need to handle safety and security-related issues.

IHS Training LLC provides the following training courses:

Safety and Security for Corporate Executives and Business Travelers – This is a half-day seminar designed to fit into most people's busy schedules. Travel Safety and Security for business trips provides specific safety and security information for virtually every aspect of your travels for business or pleasure, from what to pack to how to avoid being kidnapped. Everything in this seminar is need-to-know information and can greatly improve the chances that nothing will happen during your foreign travels. The information is provided in a very upbeat and positive manner with the goal being to encourage people to travel and work overseas.

Travel Safety and Security for Mission Trips and Missionaries – IHS Training offers our Travel Safety and Security seminar in a format specifically designed for people traveling on church mission trips or for people moving into full-time missionary positions. This seminar includes a biblical perspective on safety and security.

Crisis Management and Disaster Planning – This is a one-day, all-day course for churches, organizations, government and corporate personnel who may be called to manage a major crisis event. If you send multiple teams or personnel out of the country or you are involved in any relief-type efforts, this course will teach your personnel how to manage a major crisis situation. You'll learn how to determine what events you are prepared for, everything from an active shooter inside your facility to a natural disaster, and where your efforts to prepare for these events need to be directed. You'll learn how to avoid making the same fatal errors and mistakes other organizations have made in the past. This course includes extensive table-top exercises with a team-building approach. Be prepared to put your thinking caps on and find out whether your current policies and procedures can handle a major crisis.

Basics of Survival Training – Just like the information presented in this book, IHS Training provides straight-forward, practical instruction on survival and teaches practical skills that will keep victims alive in a survival situation.

There are all sorts of companies out there teaching survival training. Some are good and some are not! Many follow the latest trend in following dramatic survival shows on TV and provide information on survival techniques that, if followed, can get someone in serious trouble or even killed during an actual survival situation. Let's face it the fastest way to the bottom of a mountain is not by climbing down an ice cold creek and repelling through a waterfall. That may be exciting for TV but in reality it is the fastest way to become hypothermic.

Most rescues happen within the first 48 to 72 hours after a person goes missing. A surprising number of people don't make it through these first few days. Our survival courses teach skills that just about anyone can learn within a few hours. These are skills that can literally keep you alive until you can be rescued!

Active Shooter in the Workplace / Church – This course provides critical information to companies, organizations or churches on how to properly handle an active shooter event. A lot of entities are still following the old "Lock Down" procedure as the only response to an active shooter event which often results in deadly consequences. After the attack on Columbine, experts in this field realized that the procedures followed by both, the people inside the building and by law enforcement were wrong! After Columbine everything changed.

This active shooter course covers: myths and misconceptions, statistics, situational awareness, identifying suspicious activity, proper response to an active shooter event, first responder issues, use of force, dealing with the media and managing the aftermath.

Airline Crewmember Security Training – This course is designed specifically for airline employees. It covers the FAA and TSA requirements for initial and recurrent crewmember security training. This course includes a full day of instruction on regulation issues, threat evaluations, statistics, passenger issues, flight deck security, legal authority, law enforcement personnel, terrorism, attacks on aviation, trends and intelligence, bomb threats, hijacking, crewmember security off duty, and self-defense. This course is specific to FAR part 121 and 135 personnel.

BOOKS

IHS Training offers the following educational books:

"Open My Eyes" was written to provide practical advice and specific information to people traveling on church mission trips or to full-time missionaries on what to do in order to keep themselves and their traveling companions safe, as well as how to avoid trouble when traveling around the world. The advice in this book applies as much to everyday life as it does to foreign travel. The book is intended to open your eyes to the dangers that exist so that, when you are confronted with these dangers, you will automatically identify and react to them.

"Business Travel Safety" covers the exact same material found in "Open My Eyes" in a format that is designed specifically for corporate executives, business travelers and personal vacationers. It simply excludes any religious or biblical material. The corporate version of the book is entitled "Business Travel Safety." This book provides the information you need in order to keep yourself safe in today's world.

More information regarding out training courses can be found on our website: **www.IHS-Training.com**

If you are interested in booking any of our seminars or training courses, please contact us at:

info@ihs-training.com

or give us a call at: **(256) 293-7093**

IHS Training LLC

TRAVEL SAFETY & SECURITY TRAINING
EMERGENCY ACTION PLAN

IHS Training provides the following Training Aid as an
example of items to complete and/or consider when making
an Emergency Plan for foreign travel. This is only an
example and may not be inclusive of everything required
for an Emergency Plan for the location you intend to visit.
Travelers should/must research all available options and
gain any and all pertinent information before leaving the
country.

Destination City: _____ **Country:** _____

Flight Information					
Departure Date		Airline		Flight No.#	
Return Date		Airline		Flight No.#	

Hotel	
Address:	
Phone Number:	Dates

2nd Hotel	
Address:	
Phone Number:	Dates

Embassy or Consulate	
Address:	
Phone Number:	

Print Map showing Airport, Hotel, Work location and Embassy/Consulate
www.googlemaps.com and **www.bing.com/maps/**

TRAVELER INFORMATION

Name			
Address			
Phone Number		Date of Birth	
Passport Information	Number	Place of Issue	
	Date of Issue	Expiration Date	
Email Address		Citizenship	
Spouse or Contact		Phone Number	
Medical Issues			
Medications			

COMPANION INFORMATION

Name			
Address			
Phone Number		Date of Birth	
Passport Information	Number	Place of Issue	
	Date of Issue	Expiration Date	
Email Address		Citizenship	
Spouse or Contact		Phone Number	
Medical Issues			
Medications			

WORK SITE

Address:	
Phone Number:	

OTHER LOCATIONS BEING VISITED

Address:			
Phone Number:		Dates	

NEAREST HOSPITAL

Address:	
Phone Number:	

NEAREST POLICE STATION

Address:	
Phone Number:	

256

EMERGENCY EVACUATION PLAN

If something goes wrong the plan is to meet at:

PRIMARY EMERGENCY MEETING LOCATION	
Address:	
Phone Number:	

SECONDARY EMERGENCY MEETING LOCATION	
Address:	
Phone Number:	

SECONDARY COUNTRY EMBASSY or CONSULATE	
Address:	
Phone Number:	

SECONDARY COUNTRY HOW TO GET THERE	
Directions:	

EVACUATION ROUTE MAP

TRAVEL WARNINGS
Official Travel Warnings: http://travel.state.gov/travel/cis_pa_tw/tw/tw_1764.html

Registering your trip with the US Department of State

PURPOSE: To notify American citizens in the event of a disaster, emergency or other crisis, and for evacuation coordination. The information solicited may be made available as a routine use to appropriate agencies whether federal, state, local, or foreign, to assist the Department in the evacuation or provision of emergency service to US citizens.

Registration Internet Address:

https://step.state.gov/step/

CONTACT INFORMATION	
Medical Insurance Company	
Policy Number	
International Phone Number	
Credit Card Company	
Card Number	
International Phone Number	

IHS TRAINING LLC
www.IHS-Training.com

References

Pg. 28   www.fuelthemission.org

Pg. 32   CDC Report to Travel Clinics - www.cdc.gov

Pg. 33   Overseas Development Council - www.odi.org

Pg. 33   Relief Web International database -
          www.aidworkersecurity.org/incidents

Pg. 38   Child Hope International - www.childhope.org

Pg. 47   U.S. Dept. of State, official travel warnings -
          www.travel.state.gov

Pg. 53   World Health Organization - www.who.int and
          Center for Disease Control - www.cdc.gov

Pg. 57   Emergency Response International –
          www.eri-online.com

Pg. 57   LifeStraw products - www.lifestraw.com

Pg. 65   Electronic Aircraft Passenger Information
          System - www.eapis.cbp.dhs.gov

Pg. 66   www.pcworld.com/article/147739/article.html

Pg. 69   National Transportation Safety Board (NTSB) -
          www.ntsb.gov

Pg. 72   Federal Aviation Regulations 121.333, 135.89
          and 91.211

Pg. 76   Survival Phycology by Dr. John Leach,
          University of Lancaster

Pg. 76   NTSB Report -
          www.ntsb.gov/investigations/AccidentReports/P
          ages/AAR9006.aspx

Pg. 82   Civil Aero Medical Institute -
          www.faa.gov/about/office_org/headquarters_offi
          ces/avs/offices/aam/cami/

Pg. 83   www.newrichmond-news.com/content/father-
          and-son-amery-die-guatemalan-air-crash

Pg. 85   ww.usatoday30.usatoday.com/news/world/2008-
          04-15-2827678812_x.htm

Pg. 103   The Gift of Fear by Gavin de' Becker

Pg. 111   National Fire Prevention Agency report and
          video www.nfpa.org

Pg. 140   www.en.wikipedia.org/wiki/Death_by_coconut

Pg. 145   Statistic reported by Carl Chinn -
          www.carlchinn.com

Pg. 145   U.S. Bureau of Labor Statistics -
          www.bls.gov/iif/oshwc/cfoi/osar0016.htm

Pg. 148   Federal Bureau of Investigations video -
          www.fbi.gov/about-us/office-of-partner-
          engagement/active-shooter-incidents/run-hide-
          fight-video

Pg. 149   www.cnn.com/videos/world/2015/11/14/
            bataclan-concert-hall-hostages-flee-
            video.cnn/video/playlists/paris-shootings/

Pg. 150   Sandy Hook Elementary shooting statistics -
            www.en.wikipedia.org/wiki/Sandy_Hook_Eleme
            ntary_School_shooting

Pg. 151   Columbine by Dave Cullen

Pg. 152   Emanuel AME Church shooting statistics -
            www.en.wikipedia.org/wiki/Charleston_church_
            shooting

Pg. 155   Evil Invades Sanctuary by Carl Chinn

Pg. 164   www.jrcinsurancegroup.com/life-insurance-for-
            world-traveller/

Pg. 173   United Nations Office of Drug and Crime -
            www.unodc.org

Pg. 181   www.cnn.com/2010/CRIME/05/17/haiti.silsby.feeed

Pg. 187   www.nytimes.com/2010/05/02/nyregion/02times
            square.html?pagewanted=all&_r=0

Pg. 193   www.cbsnews.com/feature/tragedy-at-fort-hood/

Pg. 193   www.fbi.gov/about-us/history/famous-
            cases/oklahoma-city-bombing

Pg. 197   www.legacy.9news.com/story/news/local/
            2015/04/23/okc-bombing-luke-franey/26253625/

Pg. 198   www.en.wikipedia.org/wiki/2012_Benghazi_
           attack

Pg. 200   Aid Worker Security Report -
           www.aidworkersecurity.org/sites/default/files/Ai
           dWorkerSecurityReport_2013_web.pdf

Pg. 201   Amnesty International - www.amnestyusa.org

Pg. 202   Overseas Security Advisory Council -
           www.osac.gov

Pg. 202   U.S. Department of State Foreign Affairs Manual
           www.fam.state.gov

Pg. 211   www.politifact.com/texas/statements/2010/
           jun/28/john-mccain/mccain-says-phoenix-
           second-kidnapping-capital-worl/

Pg. 216   In the Presence of my Enemies
           by Gracia Burnham

Pg. 227   Out of Captivity by Marc Gonsalves,
           Keith Stansell and Tom Howes

Pg. 228   www.medical-dictionary.thefreedictionary.com/
           Stockholm+syndrome

Pg. 238   Lynn University report - www.lynn.edu/haiti

Pg. 243   IHS Training LLC - www.ihs-training.com

Pg. 247   www.biblestudytools.com/commentaries/
           gills-exposition-of-the-bible/matther-10-16.html